The Vegetable Garden Displayed

WITH OVER TWO HUNDRED PHOTOGRAPHS

THE ROYAL HORTICULTURAL SOCIETY
VINCENT SQUARE LONDON

Foreword and Acknowledgments

It is forty years since *The Vegetable Garden Displayed* was first published. In the intervening years it has been a guide to generations of beginners and a reminder to more experienced gardeners to the art and science of growing vegetables on a small scale.

Three years ago it was felt that it was time to revise the text once more and to take new pictures. The original purpose of the book was not to be changed – to get as much produce from a given area of the garden or allotment, as efficiently as possible, over as long a period as possible while maintaining the fertility of the soil. But the coverage of the book has now been extended to include the use of cloches and low plastic tunnels for protecting crops, as well as for raising young plants. Additional crops have been described which would have been classed as rare or unusual forty years ago. A colour section illustrating some of the major pests and diseases has also been added, to help in their identification.

We were very fortunate to get Joy Larkcom to write the text from the beginning for her knowledge and experience of growing vegetables for home supplies was perfect for the project. We have also had very valuable comment on the text from staff at the National Vegetable Research Station (Wellesbourne, Warwickshire), headed by the Director, Professor J. K. A. Bleasdale. The final text is, however, the responsibility of the R.H.S.

A third source of valuable experience has been Mr B. Doe, vegetable trials foreman at the R.H.S. Garden, Wisley, who was instrumental in the preparation for the photography at the Garden. He, too, made valuable comments on the text.

Other most welcome help with the text was given by Dr K. R. Gray of the Department of Chemical Engineering, University of Birmingham, on compost, by Dr T. J. Cleaver of the N.V.R.S. on the table of nitrogen fertilizers for vegetables, and by Mr W. Chowings of the National Institute of Agricultural Botany, Cambridge, and Mr L. J. Beavan of Hursts on vegetable varieties. Miss Brooks and Mr Halstead (of the R.H.S. Garden) made valuable comments on the pest and disease section.

The photography was cheerfully undertaken by Mr L. Hammett of the Harry Smith Horticultural Photography Collection, who made regular visits to the R.H.S. Garden at Wisley for this purpose during the season.

Designed by Julian Holland

First published 1941
Completely revised and rewritten 1981
Published by The Royal Horticultural Society

ISBN 0906 603 161

Contents

Introduction

The aim of this publication is to provide a simple but authoritative guide on vegetable growing for amateurs, particularly for those who are new to gardening. The text of *The Vegetable Garden Displayed* was first published in 1941 to meet the needs of a nation at war and has been revised and reprinted through many editions since then. Needless to say, there have been tremendous changes in vegetable growing in the last 20 years and in this edition, for which the text has again been completely rewritten, we have tried to take these changes into account.

Perhaps the most significant change is that while more people may be growing their own vegetables, the size of the average vegetable garden has shrunk. Large private vegetable gardens have become rarities, and their place has been taken by far smaller plots. Allotments, to cope with the increased demand, are now often divided to half their original size. So wherever vegetables are being grown for home consumption, the owners are concerned to get as much produce as they can out of the area available to them. In this edition of *The Vegetable Garden Displayed*, therefore, we lay more emphasis on intensive, space saving and productive methods.

Reflecting these trends a new section on 'protected cropping' has been added, covering the use of cloches and low polythene tunnels, all of which have an important role to play in extending the growing season for vegetables and increasing yields from a small area.

Another new feature is a section on raising plants indoors, to give them an earlier start. The use of soil blocks has been included, a technique particularly suited to the smaller, modern vegetable garden where only relatively few plants, though perhaps of a wide range of crops, are required.

Fashions come and go in vegetables as in all spheres of human activity, and while some vegetables, seakale for example, have fallen from favour in recent years, others have taken their place. Many more amateurs are growing vegetables previously considered exotic, such as sweet peppers, aubergines, fennel and garlic. These are included in *The Vegetable Garden Displayed* for the first time.

A number of less exotic but nevertheless useful vegetables have also crept quietly into our kitchen gardens, most notable perhaps Chinese cabbage. Many amateurs have found it a very useful autumn crop. The Abyssinian cabbage 'Karate' is another recently introduced vegetable, valuable particularly for spring greens; and while ordinary garden peas may be on the decline as they frequently give poor returns for the space they occupy, their more productive cousins, sugar peas, in which the whole pod is edible, are becoming increasingly popular.

The exorbitant cost of heating greenhouses and frames these days may lead to renewed interest in some of the many hardy native and foreign plants which have been relatively neglected in recent years: lamb's lettuce or corn salad, land cress, winter purslane, various endives, and Witloof, Sugar Loaf and the colourful red-leaved chicories. All have the merit of being extremely easy to grow and some also utilize ground which in many gardens is idle during the winter.

On the other hand, as this is essentially a basic handbook, the use of greenhouses and walk-in polythene tunnels for vegetables is omitted. Nor is there any mention of growing vegetables for showing: for both these fields specialist texts must be consulted.

The last 30 years have seen a great deal of research into commercial vegetable production, spear-headed in this country by the National Vegetable Research Station (NVRS) at Wellesbourne. Many of the research findings are applicable to amateur vegetable growers, some of them almost revolutionary in their implications. This is particularly true of work on spacing, sowing, planting and watering, but to a lesser extent applies also to plant nutrition and pest and disease control. In the book *Know & Grow Vegetables* (1979 and 1982, Oxford University Press) various members of the staff at the NVRS discuss this work and its bearing on vegetable growing on a domestic scale. Extensive use has been made of their recommendations in this revision of *The Vegetable Garden Displayed*.

The most challenging of these new ideas is the concept of equidistant spacing between plants. For some centuries now we have grown vegetables in rows that are relatively widely spaced. *Within* each row individual plants compete for nutrients, water and light, while *between* rows, the weeds, having no competition, flourish. In practice plants take their requirements for food and water from only a relatively small circular area around them, and the most productive means of using ground is to space plants an equal distance apart, planted so that when mature the leaves just touch.

In commercial vegetable growing this idea has been translated into the 'bed system'. Plants are grown relatively close together in narrow beds, separated by permanent paths which are designed for tractors. This system can easily be adapted to gardens, making beds 3 to 4 feet wide (0.9–1.2 m), with paths between. Besides giving high yields, the bed system has several other advantages. First, one only cultivates and manures ground which is actually used for growing, so there is no waste of resources or effort. Second, the soil is worked from the paths so there is never any need to tread on it, which always damages the soil structure. Third, most crops when mature (narrow-leaved plants like onions are an exception) form a canopy over the soil, excluding the light below, so largely preventing weeds from germinating and growing. The weeds in the paths can easily be controlled with weedkillers or by mulching with, for example, sawdust. Although conventional spacing in rows is generally recommended in the following pages, alternative suggestions for closer or equidistant spacing are given for certain crops.

There is considerable variation in climate throughout the British Isles, and no recommendations for the timing of sowing, planting, or any other operations apply to the whole country. Those given in *The Vegetable Garden Displayed* are generally appropriate for average conditions in the south of England. As a rule, spring operations are carried out *later* in the north, on exposed sites, and on wet heavy soils, and *earlier* in mild coastal areas, sheltered gardens, and on exceptionally light soils. Conversely autumn operations are carried out earlier in less favoured regions and sites. However, garden operations should never be carried out by the calendar: one should be guided *primarily* by the state of the soil and prevailing weather conditions.

It is very useful to keep brief records of operations in the kitchen garden. In the long run they often provide the most reliable guidance on what to do, when, and in what quantities, for one's own requirements and circumstances. It is unwise to rely on one's memory.

THE BED SYSTEM

A close-up of the carrot bed shows that weed growth has been suppressed.

Beetroot and carrots grown in close rows soon cover the soil.

Soil fertility

Soil fertility is indisputably the key to successful vegetable growing, and consciously or unconsciously, the efforts of good gardeners are always directed towards improving the fertility of their soil. There is no precise definition of fertile soil, but the following are its characteristics: it has a good crumbly structure, is rich in nutrients (plant foods), is well drained but retains a reasonable amount of moisture, and is slightly acid or neutral.

One of the soil's most important functions is its role as a reservoir of the mineral nutrients a plant needs. These are taken in by the roots, dissolved in water. Some, such as nitrogen, phosphorus, potassium, calcium, magnesium and sulphur, known as the major elements, are required in relatively large quantities; while others, the minor or trace elements, are only needed in very small quantities. These include iron, manganese, boron, zinc, copper, and molybdenum.

All these elements are released naturally by the weathering of the mineral particles in the soil and by the breakdown or decay of organic matter and humus. Nitrogen is also obtained from the air in the soil, converted into forms suitable for plant use by bacteria, including the nitrogen-fixing bacteria on the root nodules of leguminous plants. Other micro-organisms are responsible for breaking down the organic matter and humus in the soil so that nutrients can be released from it. However, these micro-organisms can only operate when they have adequate supplies of oxygen and water – an important reason why fertile soils must have a good structure.

Soil structure

Structure is determined by the soil 'crumbs', the small lumps of soil which cannot be broken down by hand. They consist of mineral and organic particles joined together. In a good soil the crumbs vary in size, and between them and around them a network of spaces and pores is built up which forms the soil structure. The channels made by these spaces and pores act as the aeration and drainage system of the soil: excess water drains off through the large pores preventing waterlogging, but is held in the smallest pores, which act as a reservoir. The larger pores then fill with air, supplying the oxygen which is essential both for the plant roots and for the living organisms in the soil.

The crucial difference between the different types of soil encountered in gardens is their ability to form crumbs. At one extreme are the clays, made up of tiny particles which stick together to form impenetrable clods. At the other are sandy soils, composed of large particles reluctant to join together to form crumbs. Silty soils have intermediate sized particles, and some of the characteristics of clays and sands. Clay soils, although slow to warm up in spring, are apt to become waterlogged and airless, but have the potential of a good structure; sandy soils are well drained, airy, and quick to warm up in spring but it is often difficult to improve their structure. The ideal garden soil is a balanced mixture of clay, sand and silt.

For all soils, the main agent for improving the structure of soil is humus. Not only is it a source of nutrients but it is able both to coat particles of sand and silt so that they adhere together to form crumbs; and to help in the breakdown of large clay clods into smaller clods, which in turn break down into crumbs. Besides these qualities, it has a great capacity for increasing the amount of water held in the soil. Humus is obtained by the breakdown of organic matter, and the regular incorporation of organic matter into all types of soils will help to improve their structure and water-holding ability.

Forms of organic matter

Organic matter is anything of animal or vegetable origin which will rot down. The forms of bulky farmyard manures traditionally used in vegetable gardens are now scarce. They are best when mixed with plenty of straw and litter, and should not be used fresh, as they may scorch plants, cause root crops such as parsnips to fork, and may contain soil pests and weed seeds. Where well-rotted manure cannot be obtained, manures should be composted for at least 6 months before use, to reduce the problems.

Some modern substitutes for farmyard manure are spent mushroom compost, treated sewage sludge (if guaranteed free of toxic metal contents), municipal waste and slaughter house waste, but there are many others sold for use in gardens.

Seaweed is an excellent form of manure; so is well-made compost – though it is not easy to make large enough quantities for most gardens. (For compost making see pp. 12–14.) Straw is a good source of organic matter, but needs to be composted before use, otherwise during decomposition it robs the soil of nitrogen. Incorporating peat into very heavy, very light and chalky soils helps to improve the soil structure. Use a layer at least an inch thick (2.5 cm).

Bulky organic matter is most effective when thoroughly mixed into the soil. NVRS recommends a minimum rate for farmyard manure of at least 10 lb/sq. yd (5.4 kg/m^2) per year to improve soils with poor structure. Garden compost (which contains less water) can also be added at 5 to 10 lb/sq. yd (2–5.4 kg/m^2). It should be mixed throughout the soil, rather than laying it at the bottom of a trench – the traditional practice. It should also be worked as *deeply* into the soil as feasible, as vegetable roots can penetrate several feet deep in favourable conditions, so drawing nutrients and moisture from lower levels. Deep rooting should be encouraged as a good insurance against the effects of drought.

The incorporation of organic matter into the soil encourages the worm population. Worms improve soil fertility by breaking up clods with their tunnelling, so improving aeration and drainage. This tunnelling also encourages deeper root penetration. Root growth is easily impeded by mechanical barriers, but roots will grow more quickly along earthworm tunnels than in unworked soil.

Organic matter can also be spread on the surface in a layer up to 3 to 4 inches deep (10 cm), either allowing the worms to work it in, or eventually forking it into the surface. This is easier than digging it in several inches down, but the humus will not be so well distributed throughout the rooting area. Light soils especially benefit by being covered with organic matter during the winter, forking it in in spring.

Generally speaking, most organic matter breaks down and disappears fairly quickly, so if possible some should be worked into the soil each year. The nutrient content of bulky organic manures is low, and on less fertile soils needs to be supplemented by artificial fertilizers to obtain worthwhile yields.

Green manuring

Green manuring is a technique of growing a crop which is dug into the soil to improve soil fertility. Some green manures are used primarily to increase the nitrogen in the soil, others to increase the organic matter in the soil. For nitrogen, fast-growing, leafy crops such as mustard and rape are used for an immediate increase, and leguminous crops with nitrogen-fixing root nodules (clovers, vetches, winter tares, lupins, beans), for a slower, long-term release of nitrogen. Plants with a fibrous root system such as annual rye grass are particularly valuable for increasing the organic matter in the soil.

Green manures are broadcast when a plot of land becomes vacant, being dug in several weeks or months later as appropriate. It is not always easy to work a green manure into the cropping plan of an intensively used vegetable garden, and certain factors have to be taken into consideration. (For example mustard and rape should not be grown on soil infected with clubroot as they belong to the cabbage family.) For further information on the use of green manures specialist texts should be consulted.

Making a start on poor soil
When starting to cultivate very poor soil it is advisable to concentrate available organic matter into relatively small areas, for the first sowings or plantings. For example, fertile 'pockets' can be created by making small trenches up to 6 inches deep (15 cm), filled with commercial potting compost or well-rotted garden compost, and covered with an inch or so of a soil and compost mixture. Here spring onions, radishes, carrots, dwarf beans or lettuce could be sown.

Potatoes and jerusalem artichokes are also useful crops to plant on poor, roughly cultivated ground: they help to break up the soil and so start to improve soil structure. Indeed, soil structure tends to improve simply as a result of the ground being cultivated and cropped, not least because the plant roots help to build up the organic matter.

Preserving the soil structure
Improving soil fertility is bound to be a gradual process, but care must be taken not to undo the good work by destroying soil structure. Never cultivate the soil when it is very wet or very dry, and avoid treading on cultivated ground: these are all processes which tend to destroy the soil structure.

Heavy rain beating on bare soil has the same effect. For this reason most soils benefit from being permanently covered – with a growing crop, with a mulch, or even with weeds, provided they are dug in before seeding. An exception is very heavy soil which benefits from exposure to frosts in winter.

Drainage
Poor drainage is a common cause of infertility; waterlogged soils are airless and cold. Signs of poor drainage are often obvious, such as water lying on the surface several days after rain, or lying permanently within, say a foot of the surface (30 cm). Poor vegetation, no earthworms, small shallow roots rather than deep roots, and greyish, bluish or mottled rather than brown soil are other signs of bad drainage.

The problem may be caused by the poor nature of the top soil – a good example is clay soil with little humus in it. Sometimes it is caused by an underlying layer of impervious subsoil or rock, or even a compacted layer in the soil. This must be broken up with a spade or pickaxe.

Forking in plenty of bulky organic manure, which will absorb a great deal of water and encourage worm activity, goes a long way towards improving a drainage problem. Where the problem is more persistent, simple trench drains can be dug in a garden, either across the lower end of a slope, or on either side of a level site. A trench about a foot wide and 2 to 3 feet deep is taken out (30 x 80–90 cm), and the bottom half filled with rubble such as stones, clinkers and broken bricks, before replacing the soil. Such a trench will in most cases absorb surplus water and render the soil more workable.

Where waterlogging is very serious it may be necessary to lay a permanent system of herring-bone drains throughout the garden, with clay or plastic pipes in the drains. The whole system needs to be designed to drain away either to a natural outlet such as a ditch, or to an artificial soakaway.

DRAINAGE

A trench, 2 to 3 feet deep, half-filled with stones, and then with earth, will help a persistent drainage problem.

Soil acidity

Soil infertility may also be due to a soil being too acid or too alkaline. Soil acidity/alkalinity is measured on the pH scale, which broadly speaking, reflects the amount of calcium in the soil. Neutral point on the scale is 7, soils with a pH below 7 becoming progressively more acid, and those above 7 progressively more alkaline.

Most soils in this country have a pH in the range of 4.5 to 7.5. The pH level can be measured reasonably accurately with a soil test kit. It is well known that certain plants prefer certain pH levels – rhododendrons, for example, only do well on acidic soils. Most vegetables prefer a slightly acid soil (around pH 6.5) although on organic (i.e. peaty) soils, they will tolerate a lower pH than on normal 'mineral' soils.

Soils in the British Isles tend to become acid, as rainwater is continually washing calcium out of the soil. This is accentuated in industrial areas, due to the acids in the atmosphere, and on light sandy soils. Heavy, clay soils may have enough calcium reserves to replenish that leached out.

Correcting acidity

Acidity is corrected by applying lime, but there has been a tendency in the past to apply lime whether or not the soil needs it, resulting in over-liming. This has harmful effects on plant growth as it suppresses the availability of minor nutrients. Where crops are growing well it is safe to assume there is no need to lime: but where crop growth is poor, where the soil has a somewhat sour look with moss growing on the surface, where vegetation is not decaying or where weeds such as sorrel and docks predominate, lime is probably needed. This can be confirmed with a soil test.

The pH of an acid soil can be raised only gradually. The aim should be to raise it to a level of 6.5 with several annual dressings of lime. Lime is best applied to the surface in the autumn, before digging, ideally on ground which will subsequently be planted with a lime-loving crop such as brassicas. The rate of the dressing depends on the nature of the soil and its present pH. The modern recommendation is to apply ground limestone at the following rates:

Sandy soil: ½ lb/sq. yd (270 g/m²)
Loamy soil: 1 lb/sq. yd (550 g/m²)
Clay or humus-rich soil: 1½ lb/sq. yd (800 g/m²)

These rates are for soils with moderate acidity (pH 6). More acid soils need larger quantities of lime.

Certain plant diseases are accenuated by pH level; clubroot in brassicas is more serious in acidic soils, and potato scab in alkaline soils.

When applying lime to the soil do not incorporate it at the same time as manure or fertilizers containing ammonia. The reaction between the two will cause the escape of ammonia as a gas without benefiting the crop.

Correcting over-alkalinity

The problem of an (naturally) over-alkaline soil is rare, and more difficult to correct. Acid peat can be worked into the soil; or powdered sulphur or ferrous sulphate applied at the rate of 4 oz/sq. yd (130 g/m²): ammonium nitrate will also reduce the pH level. In a very alkaline garden avoid using fertilizers such as Nitrochalk, which contain calcium. It may be necessary to avoid growing crops such as potatoes and rhubarb which require acidic conditions. Problems of excess acidity or alkalinity are less likely to arise in soils to which humus is regularly applied.

Supplying the nutrients

Although many people obtain adequate vegetable crops from gardens where extensive use is made of compost and manure, in most cases higher yields can be obtained by the supplementary application of artificial fertilizers.

The three major nutrients are nitrogen, phosphorus and potassium, and most artificial fertilizers supply one of these. Some supply two or more. The plant can only take up the chemicals in certain forms, so the content of available nutrient is quoted on the bag or label, as % N for nitrogen, % P_2O_5 for phosphate, and % K_2O for potash. Contents vary considerably and it is important to know how much of each nutrient is being applied.

In theory the amount of each nutrient required depends on the crop to be grown and the amounts already present in the soil.

It is unfortunately not easy for amateurs to get a nutrient analysis of their soil, but it is known that nitrogen is very mobile in the soil and is easily washed out of the soil during the winter. Phosphate and potash are relatively immobile and residues of one year's application will remain in the root area for more than one season. It has been calculated that just under ½ oz each/sq. yd (15 g/m^2) of phosphate and potash are needed each year to maintain adequate levels in the soil for vegetables (requirements are the same for all). This amount can be satisfactorily supplied by the annual incorporation suggested on p. 7 of farmyard manure at 10 lb/sq. yd (5.4 kg/m^2) or good garden compost at 5 to 10 lb/sq. yd (2–5.4 kg/m^2).

They can also be supplied by applying 2 oz of superphosphate per square yard (66 g/m^2) and 1 oz of sulphate of potash per square yard (33 g/m^2) each year. Additional humus must also be worked in. The time of application is not important, but can be most conveniently done in autumn.

Wherever possible it is advisable to have the soil analysed at intervals of about five years to check that levels of available phosphate and potash are adequate.

The nitrogen requirement of different vegetables varies considerably, and as has already been stated the soil content of nitrogen is regularly reduced during the winter. So nitrogen needs to be supplied annually to obtain good crops. Later in the text the terms base-dressing and top-dressing are used in relation to fertilizer application. The base-dressing refers to application before sowing, and the top-dressing to application after the crop is established and growing vigorously.

Vegetables can be grouped roughly according to their nitrogen requirements. For example, peas need no extra nitrogen; carrots and radishes have low nitrogen requirements; broad beans, parsnips, lettuces, onions, calabrese, french beans and turnips have moderate requirements; and potatoes, beetroots, spinach, cauliflowers, brussels sprouts and cabbages have high requirements for nitrogen.

The amount of nitrogen fertilizer per square yard applied annually depends on the crop and the nitrogen content of the fertilizer (quoted as % N on the bag). The table opposite gives a guide to the amount of fertilizer (six are quoted) needed by a wide range of vegetable crops. This guide assumes an average garden soil to which crop residues are regularly returned in the form of compost.

Nitrogen fertilizers may be incorporated into the soil surface, preferably a month before sowing. They *can* be mixed in just before sowing, but only if the soil is moist, and, to be safe, no more than a third of the crop's total requirement. Higher concentrations than this at an early stage of plant growth are likely to depress seedling growth and emergence. The remainder of the nitrogen needed is applied as a top-dressing once the crop is established.

Overwintered crops such as spring cabbages and autumn-sown onions need most of their nitrogen in spring, and this is applied as a top-dressing.

Artificial fertilizers

The 'straight' fertilizers supplying nitrogen include nitrate of soda, calcium nitrate, sulphate of ammonia and Nitrochalk. Nitrate of potash contains both nitrogen and potash. Nitrogen is fairly rapidly washed out of the soil, so nitrogenous fertilizers are applied for short-term use, either just before sowing or transplanting or as a top-dressing during the crop's growing season.

Fertilizers supplying phosphorus are superphosphate (20% P_2O_5) and triple superphosphate (44% P_2O_5). Phosphate from these is released into the soil much more slowly than from nitrogen fertilizers, so they are best applied well before the plants need them, e.g. in the autumn.

Fertilizers which supply potassium are sulphate of potash (49% K_2O) and nitrate of potash (36% K_2O) which also contains nitrogen. Like phosphate fertilizers they are best applied well before the growing season.

Rates of application of nitrogen fertilizer at oz. per sq. yd[1]

	Growmore[2] (7% N)	Nitrate of potash[2] (12% N)	Calcium nitrate: Nitrate of soda (15% N)	Nitrochalk: Sulphate of ammonia (21% N)
Artichokes: Globe	2	1	1	¾
Jerusalem	5	2½	2¼	1½
Asparagus: establishment	3	1¾	1½	1
cutting years	2	1	1	¾
Aubergines	2	1	1	¾
Beans: Broad	3	1¾	1½	1
French	3	1¾	1½	1
Runner	3	1¾	1½	1
Beetroots[3]	8½	4½	4	3
Brassicas: Broccoli, sprouting[3]	5	3	2½	1¾
Brussels sprouts[3]	10	5½	5	3½
Cabbage, spring[3]	10	5½	5	3½
Cabbage, summer[3]	10	5½	5	3½
Cabbage, winter[3]	10	5½	5	3½
Cabbage, winter storage[3]	5	3	2½	1¾
Calabrese[3]	5	3	2½	1¾
Cauliflower[3]	5	3	2½	1¾
Kale[3]	5	3	2½	1¾
Carrots	1	½	½	½
Celeriac	2	1	1	¾
Celery, self blanching	5	3	2½	1¾
Chicory	3	1¾	1½	1
Chinese cabbage	10	5½	5	3½
Cucumber	3	1¾	1½	1
Endive	4¼	2¼	2	1½
Florence fennel	3	1¾	1½	1
Kohl rabi	2	1	1	¾
Leeks[3]	6½	3½	3	2
Lettuces	4¼	2¼	2	1½
Marrows	3	1¾	1½	1
Onions	3⅓	1¾	1½	1
Parsnips	3	1¾	1½	1
Peas	0	0	0	0
Potatoes: Early	5	2½	2¼	1½
Maincrop	6½	3½	3	2
Radishes	1	½	½	½
Rhubarb: establishment	5	3	2½	1¾
cutting years	10	5½	5	3½
Salsify and Scorzonera	3	1¾	1½	1
Spinach[3]	4¼	2¼	2	1½
Spinach beet[3]	8½	4½	4	3
Swedes	2	1	1	¾
Sweet corn	4¼	2¼	2	1½
Sweet peppers	2	1	1	¾
Tomatoes (outdoor)	2	1	1	¾
Turnips	2	1	1	¾

[1]These figures are calculated on the assumption that organic matter is regularly incorporated into the soil (e.g. all composted waste is regularly returned to the vegetable garden, as recommended on p 7) so supplying some nitrogen, and maintaining adequate amounts of phosphate and potash in the soil.

[2]The compound fertilizers Growmore and nitrate of potash also contain other major nutrients (Growmore + 7% P_2O_5 and 7% K_2O, nitrate of potash + 60% K_2O); Nitrochalk and calcium nitrate also contain calcium.

[3]For these crops sown direct only a third of the amount of fertilizer quoted should be applied before sowing: the rest can be given after the crop is established.

Fertilizers are sold in solid forms – dusts, granules or pellets – or as concentrated liquid solutions. Dry forms are sprinkled on the surface as evenly as possible and raked or hoed in. If the ground is dry they must be watered in to dissolve the fertilizer and wash it down to the roots. Some forms of pelleted fertilizer are placed in the soil near the roots.

Liquid fertilizers are diluted and watered on the soil; they must be prepared and used according to the manufacturer's instructions. They are taken up by the plant more quickly than solid fertilizers. In addition, as plants can absorb limited amounts of nutrients through their leaves, proprietary liquid fertilizers are sometimes recommended as a foliar feed, being sprayed or watered on the leaves. This form of feeding is also useful where it is necessary to correct a nutrient deficiency, for example magnesium deficiency.

It is also possible to buy compound fertilizers already mixed to supply varying proportions of N, P_2O_5 and K_2O. Growmore (7% N:7% P_2O_5:7% K_2O) is one which is readily available – but there are others. There is however only a limited range of compound fertilizers available for gardeners. These fertilizers are easy to apply and convenient when all three nutrients are needed.

The three major nutrients can also be supplied in organic fertilizers, such as dried blood (12% N, 2·5% P_2O_5, 1% K_2O), bone meal (4% N, 7% P_2O_5), seaweed extracts (1·5% N, 5% K_2O) and hoof-and-horn (14% N, 2·5% P_2O_5). The nutrients are released relatively showly to the plants, and may not provide enough nitrogen at the right time for vegetables. These tend to be a relatively expensive way of buying nutrients.

Trace elements

Although plants require trace elements (of which there are many) in only minute quantities, the deficiency of any one of them can result in poor growth. Some crops are particularly vulnerable to certain deficiencies – cauliflower to molybdenum, for example. Once identified (a specialist task), deficiencies can be corrected by applying fertilizers containing the necessary elements, usually as a foliar feed for quick action. In practice trace-element deficiencies are most unlikely to occur on soils which have been well manured, though they may be induced by over-liming. High pH following liming is a major cause of induced trace-element deficiencies.

Compost

Compost is a valuable source of organic matter, and all serious gardeners should try to make their own. It is made by building a heap of vegetable and animal wastes, which generate heat and are rotted down by many types of micro-organisms. When compost is well made the end-product is blackish brown, moist, crumbly and uniform in texture.

Depending on the conditions, two different natural processes can be utilized to make compost: *aerobic* (requiring a free flow of air) and *anaerobic* (not requiring air). Broadly speaking, aerobic compost is made with fairly large quantities of waste in well-insulated bins with access to air, and anaerobic in sealed containers or covered piles where air is excluded.

The advantages of aerobic composting are that almost any organic material can be included; that weed seeds, roots of most perennial weeds and disease organisms are killed; that no odours are produced or flies or vermin encouraged, and that it produces homogeneous compost at an acceptable degree of acidity, so it does not require liming. The compost is ready for use in two or three months, depending on the season.

Its disadvantages are that it requires fairly careful preparation and attention, and normally a box or container; that the material must occupy a minimum volume or the heat generated is wasted, that it may require turning, and that the 'carbon/nitrogen ratio' should be roughly correct. Autumn and winter heaps are therefore likely to need an activator.

Anaerobic composting, on the other hand, requires little preparation or attention, no container, no turning, and the heap can be of any size. The carbon/nitrogen ratio is not important so no activator is required. Its drawbacks are that weed seeds, perennial weeds and diseases will not be killed, that tough material will not be broken down, and that it may produce odours and attract flies unless carefully covered. The compost may be cold, heavy and rather acid, so requiring liming. It takes about a year to produce good compost in this way, and it may not be completely decomposed. In this case large pieces of undecomposed material will have to be removed or sieved out, before use.

From this it is clear that gardeners should *aim* to make aerobic compost, which gives the best and most rapid returns. If this is difficult, perhaps because only small quantities of waste are available, it is still well worth making anaerobic compost,

COMPOST BOX

On the right, the empty box showing its well-aerated base. On the left, the full box; the front would normally be covered in with, for example, loose boards when making aerobic compost. Sacking could be used on top instead of the soil cover.

even though the process takes longer and is less efficient. Valuable material is still being made to return to the soil.

Making aerobic compost

The site. Bins should be erected in a permanent position, preferably on a soil foundation so that worms can move into the compost in the final stages. Shady corners can be utilised.

Bins. Where possible construct two bins side by side – or one bin with two, or even three, compartments, so that while one is being built up the other(s) can be maturing. Suitable dimensions for a bin are approximately 3 feet square (1 m) and about 3 feet high (1 m). The structure must be strong. At least three walls should be made of materials with good heat insulation properties, such as breeze blocks, bricks, timber or straw bales. It is useful if the front

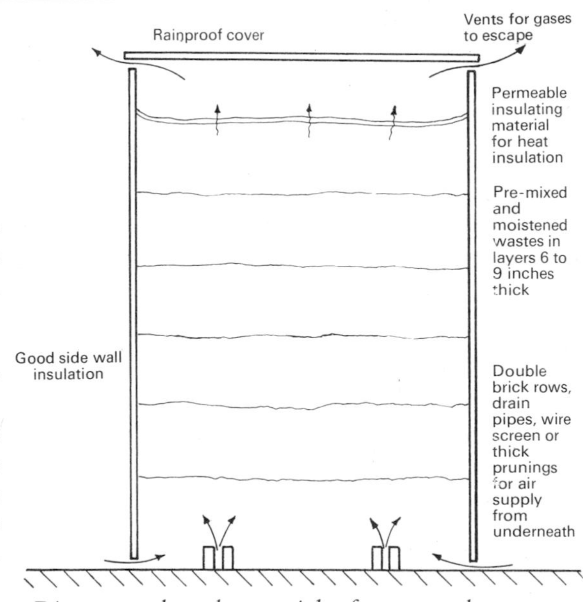

Diagram to show the essentials of a compost box

wall is either made up of loose boards, which can be slid in behind uprights, or with removable panels of timber. This makes access to the heap easier, both when it is being made and when the compost is being used. In areas of high rainfall the heap should be protected with a roof – corrugated iron is sufficient – to prevent it becoming saturated.

Building the heap. Start by forking the base soil lightly. The next step, to ensure drainage and aeration from underneath is to lay a 3 inch thick (7.5 cm) layer of brushwood or prunings on the ground. Alternatives are several rows of land drain pipes, or double rows of bricks with 2 inch gaps (5 cm) between the pairs of rows. This foundation can be covered with a strong wire screen about an inch mesh (2.5 cm) to support the compost.

The heap is best built in layers between 6 and 9 inches thick (15–22 cm). Try to accumulate enough material to make a complete layer at once, rather than adding small quantities to the heap daily. Kitchen wastes can be collected in closed plastic bags until required. Ideally the whole heap should be built in one operation.

In each layer mix the material together as thoroughly as possible before putting it in the box. Suitable garden wastes include weeds, vegetable remains, lawn mowings, leaves, old potting compost, bonfire ash, thin prunings. Nettles, comfrey and green bracken make particularly good compost. All can be mixed with kitchen waste. Paper can be used but never more than 10% by weight, and well soaked beforehand. Cut or shred thick material such as cabbage stalks and prunings into small pieces, 2 to 3 inches long (5–7.5 cm). Never make a thick layer of any one component such as grass clippings.

Perennial weeds should be killed off first by being dried in the sun. All non-rotting material should be excluded – e.g. plastics, metals, china, man-made fibres. The pre-mixed wastes should be watered, if necessary, until just damp but not sodden.

Use of activators. For optimum microbial activity the 'carbon/nitrogen ratio' of the heap needs to be roughly 30:1. (Carbon is found mainly in stems, roots and in straw; nitrogen in green leaves and manures.) In the summer months there is naturally enough leafy material in composting materials for the balance to be about right, but in autumn and winter additional nitrogen needs to be added to each layer of the heap. This can be in the form of:

- ammonium sulphate or other nitrogenous fertilizer, at about 4 oz/sq.yd (140 g/m^2)
- concentrated organic fertilizers such as dried blood, fish and bone at 8 oz/sq. yd (270 g/m^2)
- poultry or other animal manures, about 1 bucket/sq. yd or m^2
- concentrated seaweed extracts or proprietary activators as instructed by the manufacturers.

The activator should be well mixed in with the wastes before putting them into the heap.

Completing the heap. The heap is built up in layers until the top of the bin is reached, or it is between 3 and 5 feet high (1–1.5 m). To retain the heat of composting cover the top layer with a piece of plastic sheet with about 12 holes, each an inch in diameter (2.5 cm) made in it. Finally cover with some permeable insulating material such as hessian sacks, matting, old carpets or old straw.

Turning the heap. In the natural course of events the temperature in a well-made heap should rise to about 60 to 70 °C (140–158 °F) within a week and then start to fall. To speed up the composting process and to improve the kill of weed seeds, the heap can now be turned, which means rebuilding it 'sides to middle', the cooler outer layer being placed in the centre of the heap. In a compost bin with several compartments, the heap is transferred to an empty compartment. Turning is a laborious process, but there is no doubt that better compost is made if the heap can be turned once. After turning, the top layer is again covered with the plastic sheet and insulating material. Turning is less necessary when the walls of the bin have good insulating qualities.

Anaerobic composting

The simplest form of anaerobic compost heap is made by piling up wastes on the ground as they accumulate, to a height of about 5 feet (1.5 m). Keep the heap covered with a piece of black polythene sheet or fertilizer bags. This heap will take about a year to decompose.

Tools

There is no substitute for good-quality tools. Unfortunately there are many poor-quality tools on the market today, as well as various 'specialised' tools which are, in the main, useless.

Everyone has their favourite tools. What is important is to select tools which are the right weight and balance for oneself, so that they can be used without strain. Where bending is awkward, long-handled tools are a boon.

The life of tools is extended if they are well cared for. After use scrape off the soil and wipe them clean with an oily rag. Blades of spades and hoes need to be sharpened occasionally with a file and stone.

The *minimum* requirements for a small garden are a garden fork, rake, hoe and trowel. For larger gardens, the more of the following basic tools one has the better.

Spade. This is the traditional digging tool, and is also useful for moving soil, compost, etc.

Fork. This is also used for digging, especially on stony soil where the use of a spade is difficult, and for turning soil over to make it workable. Forks with four round prongs are the most generally practical; the broad-tined fork is traditionally used for potato lifting. The best spades and forks are made of stainless steel with ash handles.

Rake. The metal-pronged garden rake with a cast head is mainly used for creating a fine surface, or tilth, on a seed bed.

Cultivator. This multi-pronged tool is useful for breaking up rough soil before making a seed bed. It may have 3 or 5 prongs or more.

Hoes. The many types of hoe are used primarily for weeding, though some are also useful for earthing up and for drawing drills. The dutch or push hoe is used in a to and fro motion, the flat blade being slid under weeds to cut them off, so it must be kept sharp. The draw hoe, in which the blade is set at a right angle to the handle, is used for weeding with a chopping motion; it is also used for earthing up. There are also triangular hoes for drawing drills, and various types of hoe with serrated blades which improve their slicing action. An extremely useful hoe is the short-handled, swan-necked onion hoe, which enables one to weed very close to plants. Some hoes are made with robust fibreglass handles.

Hand trowel. This is an indispensable tool for planting. As it needs to be very strong, steel-bladed trowels with a curved shank are considered best.

Hand fork. This is useful both for weeding and for working the top surface of the soil before planting. Short and long handled forks are available.

Dibber. Although this is a traditional tool for making holes for planting, care should be taken when using it. If too smooth and deep a hole is made the plant may be left suspended in a pocket of air. It is most suited to planting leeks.

Measuring tools. A garden line of strong nylon cord on a reel facilitates planting straight rows. A rod marked out in commonly used distances, can also be used.

TOOLS FOR CULTIVATION

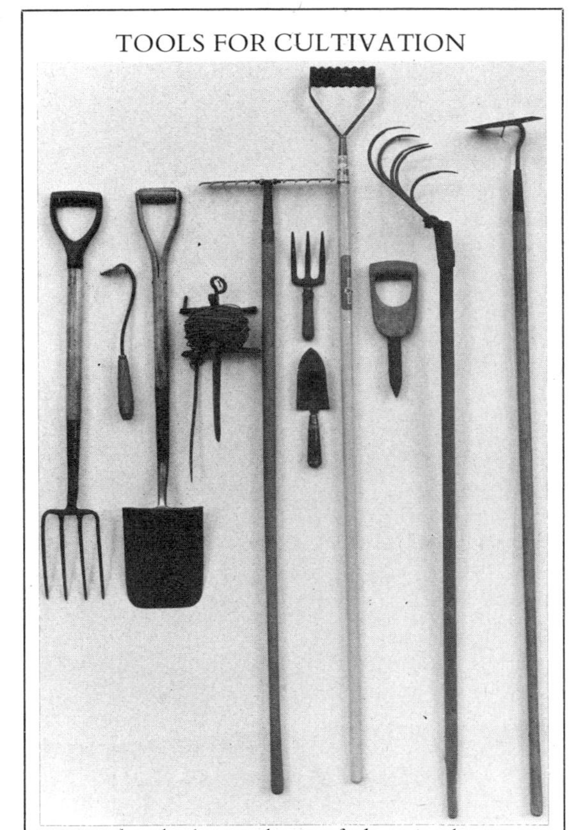

Essential tools, l. to r. digging fork, onion hoe, spade, line, rake, trowel and hand fork, push (dutch) hoe (with two-sided blade), dibber, five-pronged cultivator, draw hoe.

Watering can. A can with interchangeable fine and heavy roses is necessary. Plastic cans should be moulded in one piece, or the spout is apt to be knocked off in use. A separate can should be earmarked for application of weedkiller so that there is no danger of chemical damage to crop plants.

Sprayers. For applying pesticides on a small scale a hand syringe or hand sprayer, of $\frac{1}{2}$ to 2 pints capacity (0.28–1.25 litres) is adequate. For larger areas pressurized sprayers (with capacity ranging from 2 pints to 3 gallons (1.25–15.5 litres)) are advisable. The larger ones are either free-standing or of the knapsack type used with a long lance.

Mechanical cultivators. These are outside the scope of this book, as their purchase is probably only justified in large gardens. For smaller gardens it is more economical to hire a cultivator for the few hours' work required each year.

EQUIPMENT FOR SEED RAISING, WATERING AND SPRAYING

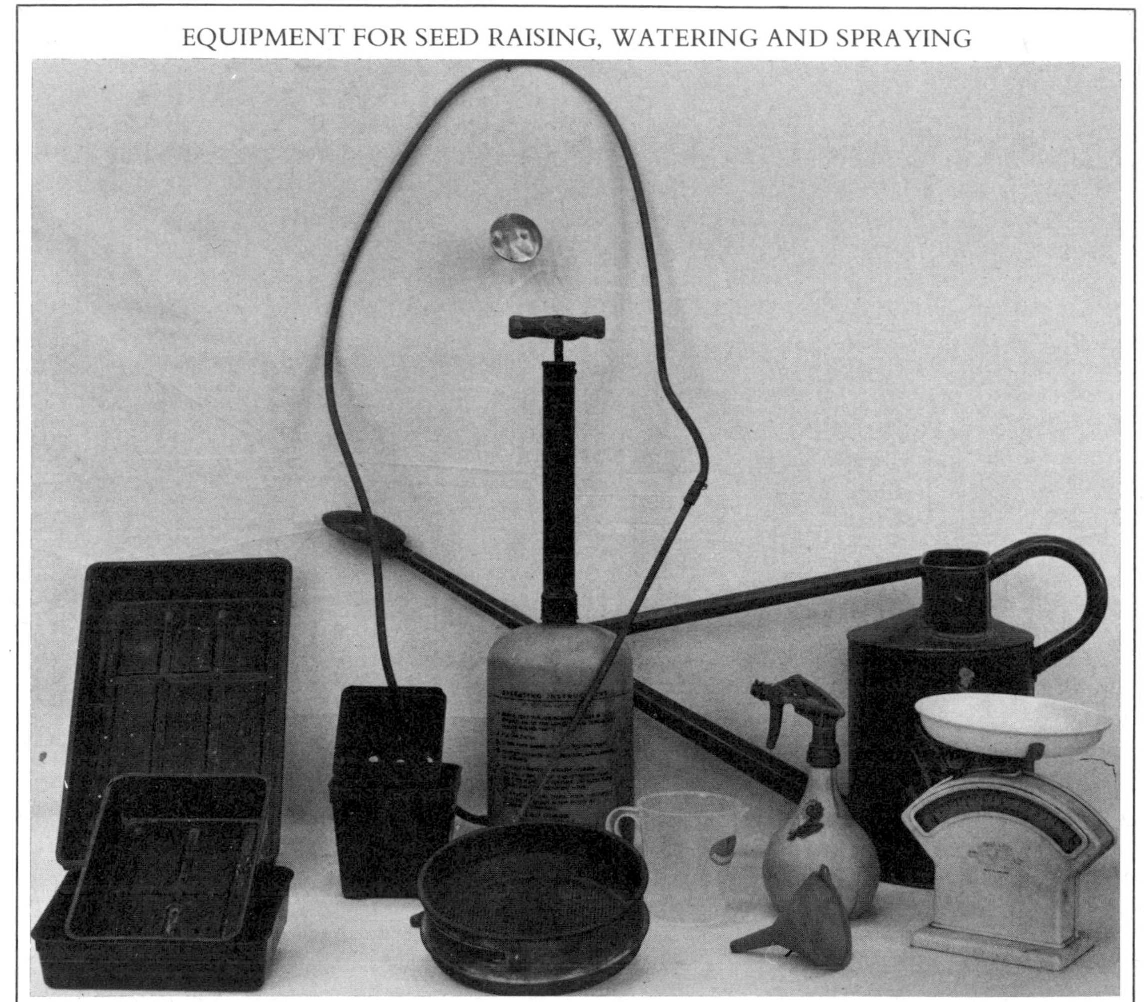

Equipment for raising seedlings (left and foreground): seed boxes, pots and a soil sieve; for spraying and watering (right and centre): pressure sprayer, hand sprayer, with jug and funnel and scales for mixing the pesticide; watering can in the background.

Soil cultivation

The purpose of digging, forking, raking and most other forms of cultivation is to get the soil into the best possible state for sowing seeds or planting. Of all these operations, digging has the most fundamental effect, in that it disturbs the soil, breaks down clods, lets in air, and provides a practical means of removing weeds and incorporating organic matter into the soil.

Digging

Digging is best carried out in the autumn or early winter on heavy soils, so that frost can break down the clods over the winter. Light soils which do not need such weathering, and may indeed lose their structure during heavy winter rains, are best left to the spring. It is practical to incorporate manure or some form of organic matter into the soil when digging.

Various systems were practised in the past.

Single digging, in which a single spit (spade's depth) was worked. The process started with making a narrow trench, which was filled with soil from the next trench.

Double digging, in which a wider trench was cut initially, and the soil in the bottom forked over thoroughly before turning in soil from the next trench.

Trenching. A big operation in which a depth of two spits was dug.

Although the modern tendency is to dig less thoroughly, recent NVRS experiments have indicated that even apparently good soil becomes compacted in the lower levels. When this compaction is broken up by deeper digging, roots penetrate more readily and extract more water from lower levels so conserving water in the upper layers. As plant nutrients are mainly in the upper layers, and can only be taken up by plants when the soil is *moist*, this benefits plant growth.

Deeper digging is not necessary every year; its effects should last for three years.

For modern gardeners, a practical compromise between the old labour-intensive forms of double digging and trenching, and the recognized need to work the soil as deeply as possible, is a halfway house between single and double digging.

The procedure is as follows:

Mark out the plot to be dug. If it is very large, divide the area into two or three sections and tackle each in turn.

Spread manure over the area to be dug to ensure even distribution. Alternatively keep it in a wheelbarrow for use as required.

Take out a trench about 15 inches (40 cm) wide and one spade deep across the plot.

Wheel this soil to the far end of the plot, or if it is divided into two then it can be laid alongside the first trench, ready for filling in the last trench.

Fork over the soil at the bottom of the trench.

Put a layer of manure in the trench.

Fork the soil and manure together, so that the manure is thoroughly spread throughout the soil.

Fill the trench with soil from the adjacent strip.

Fork over the bottom of the second trench, incorporate manure and soil from the third strip, mix them together and so on.

The last trench will be filled with the soil deposited at the end of the plot.

Lawns and grassland are sometimes converted into vegetable gardens. They are best dug in the autumn. Slice the turf off the top, and either chop it up and bury it in the bottom of the trench, or build the turves up into a separate heap, grass-side down. After a year the turves will have rotted into very useful potting soil.

Digging technique

Don't tackle too much initially as it is strenuous exercise for those unaccustomed to it.

Start by making slits in the soil at right angles to the trench: this makes it easier to remove the soil cleanly.

Always put the blade of the spade into the soil vertically, rather than at an angle, to work the ground to the maximum spade depth.

A slightly twisting motion is used so that the soil is inverted as it is put into the preceding trench.

Do not bring subsoil up to the surface as this contains very little organic matter and nutrients.

Do not break the soil up finely. It is sufficient to turn it over roughly, as frost action will break up the clods during the winter.

Never dig when the ground is very wet or there is heavy frost. Not only is this difficult to do, but it will destroy the crumb structure.

Remove roots of perennial weeds such as dock, ground elder, bindweed, dandelion, couch grass and thistles as completely as possible. Remove weeds

RECOMMENDED DIGGING METHOD

1 *The first trench dug to a spade's depth, and the soil taken to the far end of the plot.*

2 *Putting manure into the bottom of the trench.*

3 *Turning the soil from the second trench into the first, to show how the spadeful is taken.*

4 *Mixing soil and manure together, so that the manure is incorporated throughout the top soil.*

which have gone to seed and burn them; smaller weeds can be dug in.

Forking

Forking implies breaking up the top layer of soil by a digging action with a garden fork. In spring it may be all that is necessary to bring the autumn-dug soil into a workable condition.

During the growing season ground often becomes compacted and dry where a crop is grown; it may be necessary to fork over the ground between clearing one crop and sowing or planting the next.

PREPARATION FOR SOWING AND PLANTING

Forking over the soil, the first step in cultivation.

Seed

Most vegetables are raised from seeds, and it always pays to use the best quality available. Vegetable seeds sold in this country have legally to conform to minimum standards of viability (ability to germinate), cleanliness and purity, and can normally be relied upon to give good results. However, seed is grown all over the world, and inevitably the seed harvest is better in some years than others and this is reflected in the quality. Seed is also liable to deteriorate rapidly unless kept in cool dry conditions (see below): poor germination is often a result of bad storage conditions at home.

Seed merchants are only allowed to sell vegetable varieties which are on the approved National and EEC lists, which has meant the disappearance of a number of older varieties. In a few cases they are still available under another name.

Choice of cultivar

The term 'cultivar' (abbreviated as cv), which has now replaced the old term 'variety', denotes a variety raised and maintained in cultivation.

The work of plant breeders all over the world has given the modern gardener a wide choice of cultivars. Many have outstanding characteristics such as high yields, resistance to particular diseases and pests, early maturity, resistance to bolting, and compactness.

For the vegetable grower one of the most satisfactory ways of buying seed is through the mail-order seed catalogues, which frequently offer a wider choice than is normally available in shops, together with valuable information on cultivation.

The following are factors to consider in choosing a cultivar.

F_1 hybrids. These are obtained by crossing two parent lines, each of which has been inbred for several generations. Because of this the progeny has exceptional vigour and uniformity. F_1 seed is more expensive than ordinary 'open pollinated' seed, but in many cases (especially brussels sprouts and cabbages) is worth the extra cost. It is not worth saving seeds from F_1 hybrids, as they will not produce the same characters in the next generation.

Disease resistance. An increasing number of vegetable cultivars are being bred with varying degrees of resistance or tolerance to common diseases. Examples include lettuce (downy mildew), tomato (mosaic virus, leaf mould), parsnip (canker).

These cultivars are not always readily available to amateurs but it is worth looking in catalogues and considering any which are listed. The diseases themselves may eventually develop strains which overcome the resistance, so plant breeders have to be constantly producing new resistant cultivars to keep a step ahead.

Several vegetable diseases are seed borne, and seed is sometimes tested and sold as guaranteed free, or with only a very low percentage, of infected seed. (For example lettuce, tested for lettuce mosaic virus can be declared as having less than one infected seed in 30,000, i.e. less than 0.003% infected.)

Pest resistance. At the moment there are few vegetable cultivars with resistance to pests (apart from eelworm-resistant potatoes), but more are likely to be bred in future. The lettuce cvs Avoncrisp and Avondefiance have considerable resistance to lettuce root aphis.

Seed treatments for disease control. Seed can be treated or dressed with a fungicide before packaging. In some cases seed is treated against specific seed-borne diseases (e.g. celery or celeriac treated against celery leaf spot). In other cases it is treated with a fungicide such such as thiram or captan to protect seeds against general damping-off diseases, which affect them during slow germination in cold soils.

Chemically treated seed should always be handled carefully, washing the hands after sowing. Such seed must be used in the year it is bought, as its viability is likely to be affected by the treatments.

Types of seed

The most usual way of buying seeds is in a packet which contains single 'naked' seeds; in the case of beetroot, the seed is, botanically, a fruit containing several seeds. These have to be thinned on germination. Seeds are also available in other forms.

Pelleted seed. Each seed is coated with a protective substance which disintegrates in the soil. Pelleted seeds look like tiny balls, and are easier to handle, and to place precisely where required than ordinary seed, so that the need for thinning is reduced or even eliminated. However, germination problems are sometimes encountered. Pellets should be sown shallowly at about ½ inch apart (1.5 cm) and at a depth of about twice their diameter, in soil that is neither too wet nor too dry. The soil must remain moist until the seeds germinate. Gently firming the ground after sowing helps to retain soil moisture. Once these seeds have been exposed to the air they are likely to deteriorate quickly, as the material used for coating absorbs moisture from the air.

Seed tapes and 'sheets'. Individual seeds are incorporated, usually several centimetres apart, into soluble tapes or sheets of Kleenex-like paper.

These are simply laid on the seedbed or in the seed tray, and watered and covered with soil as if sowing normal seed. The seedlings, being already spaced out, do not need thinning.

Chitted seed. This is seed which has already started to germinate, and is posted to customers in tiny sachets to prevent moisture loss. Seed must be pricked out on arrival. So far only chitted seeds of cucumbers are available.

Seed quantities

Seed catalogues and packets often indicate the quantity of seed in a packet, and the length of row, or number of plants, which can be raised from it.

Seed storage

Seed deteriorates with age, progressively losing its viability and vigour, so that germination falls off and poorer crops are obtained. Deterioration is quickest when seed is kept in moist, warm conditions. (In general seed storage life is halved with each rise of 9 °F (5 °C) above 32 °F (0 °C) and with each increase in seed moisture content of 1% between 5% and 14%.) Seeds should always be stored in as cool and as dry a place as possible – never in the kitchen or a damp garden shed. It is best to store unopened seed packets in an airtight jar or tin, in which there is an open dish of cobalt-chloride-treated silica gel (obtainable from chemists and used at 1 teaspoon per oz of seed) to absorb the moisture. The gel is blue when dry, turning pink when moist. It can be dried in an oven when moist and returned to the jar or tin for further use. Most seeds stored thus will continue to germinate well for three to four years. An exception is parsnip, which cannot be relied upon for more than one season.

Seeds packed in vacuum-sealed foil packs retain their viability for three to four years, until the packet is opened, when normal deterioration begins. They too can be stored in airtight conditions with the gel as above.

Sowing

Seed germination

Seed packets contain a known percentage of seeds which are capable of germinating, but when they are sown not all will emerge as young plants. Several factors act on the seed or emerging embryo and affect its emergence.

First the condition of the soil at sowing. The technique of preparing a seedbed is described in the next section, but it is important that the soil is damp enough for the seeds to take up moisture and start the germination process.

It is also important that the soil is within the right range of temperatures for germination of the particular crop. Germination and emergence are usually less good at low rather than higher temperatures. This generally means that it is a waste of seed to sow in spring when the soil is still cold. Several vegetables, e.g. cabbages, peas and broad beans, will germinate at soil temperatures of 41 °F (5 °C) or above, others such as leeks and onions need a degree or so more (i.e. 45 °F/7 °C), and the more tropical crops, e.g. runner and french beans and cucurbits, need 65 °F (13 °C) as a minimum. There are also upper limits for some crops, e.g. butterhead lettuces, which will not germinate, or only slowly, when soil temperatures are above 77 °F (25 °C).

Depth of sowing also affects emergence. For the first few days after germination the seedlings are dependent on their own resources for food. If these are exhausted before the seedling reaches the light and can manufacture a new food supply, then the young plant will die. Small seeds, therefore, are sown nearer the soil surface than larger seeds.

Finally fertilizers. The danger of applying large amounts of certain nitrogenous fertilizers to the seedbed have already been outlined (p. 10). It is safest to apply nitrogen as a top-dressing later in the life of the crop, or alternatively place it 3 or 4 inches below the row (8–10 cm), so that it is only reached when the plants are older and less sensitive.

Testing viability

Seed bought in a previous year can be tested before sowing outdoors, by putting a few seeds on moist blotting paper in a warm place. Provided they are kept moist and reasonably warm they should germinate within 2 or 3 weeks, the first sign being the emergence of the seedling root. It should be noted that peas and beans, as well as smaller seeds, swell when moist, but this is not an indication that they are viable.

Most garden vegetables are grown from seed. Depending on the crop and its cultivation they are sown:

- outdoors where they are to grow (direct sowing)
- outdoors in close rows in a seedbed for transplanting later into their permanent positions
- under cover (usually in seed boxes, in cloches, frames or greenhouses) and later planted outside.

There are no hard and fast rules about which method to adopt. As a rough guide, direct sowing outdoors is used for plants for which transplanting is unnecessary or unlikely to succeed; difficult or laborious to transplant: for example, peas, beans, root crops such as beetroot, carrots, parsnips, radishes, turnips, and lettuces in mid-summer.

Seedbeds are used as a means of saving space, mainly for vegetables with a long growing season. Brassicas (cauliflowers, cabbages, brussels sprouts, etc.) are commonly raised in seedbeds. The ground they will eventually occupy can be used for another crop, until they are ready for transplanting.

Sowing indoors is primarily a means of avoiding adverse weather conditions early in the year. It is used for half-hardy plants such as tomatoes, cucumbers, sweet peppers and french and runner beans, which cannot be planted out until risk of frost is past; for plants which benefit from a longer growing season such as onions, leeks, celery and celeriac; and with other vegetables where earlier crops can be obtained by sowing indoors.

Sowing outdoors

Preparing the seedbed. Before sowing seeds in the open, the soil needs to be firmed but not consolidated, and the surface to be broken down and raked into what is called a 'tilth'. This implies a surface free of stones and lumps, with soil reduced to crumbs about the size of large breadcrumbs. The degree to which the crumbs are broken down depends on the size of the seeds to be sown. The smaller the seeds, the finer should the clods be broken down, so that the seeds will be in close contact with the soil and moisture, so encouraging germination. For larger seeds, e.g. peas and beans, the soil can be left rather rougher; this will discourage the germination of weed seeds.

Breaking down a rough surface into a good tilth is not always easy. A soil that has been dug over roughly in the autumn may only require a little

SOWING OUTDOORS

1 Breaking down the ground into small soil particles, using a cultivator.

2 Soil covered with clear plastic to warm the seedbed before sowing.

4 Drawing the drills to an even depth.

5 Sowing the seeds, standing on board as the ground is very wet.

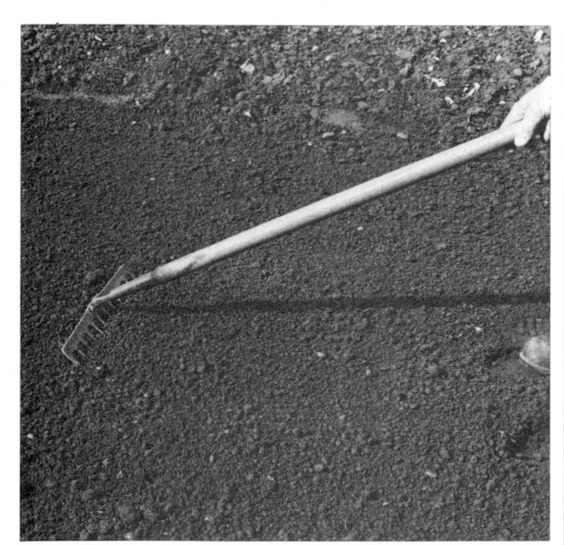

3 *Raking over the seedbed to get a level surface.*

6 *Carefully covering over the drill after sowing, with a rake.*

forking in spring, followed by raking to remove stones. But this varies with the nature of the soil. Much depends on knowing one's soil and recognizing the precise moment to start working it. Soils with plenty of organic matter in them, i.e. with a good structure, are generally easiest to work.

Soil must never be cultivated when very wet or very dry. If soil sticks to the shoes when walking on it, it is too wet. Leave it a few days more to dry out. Cloches or clear plastic can be put on the soil to help dry it out. It cannot be over-emphasized that little is gained by sowing in cold or wet soil.

If the soil is dry and dusty it will need watering before working. It is always better to water before rather than after sowing, as this helps to avoid 'capping'. This phenomenon of the surface crust drying and setting occurs on certain soils, and may prevent seedlings pushing their way through.

Some soils dry out very rapidly in spring, before one is ready to sow. A light mulch of straw or similar material on the soil, after preparing the seedbed conserves the moisture and creates a surface which can easily be raked into a good tilth just before sowing, the mulch being first raked to one side.

The traditional recommendation was to tread the seedbed before the final raking, but this is no longer generally recommended, as it may compact the soil too much. It may sometimes be necessary on the lightest of soils, on very loose soils or if the surface has become very uneven.

Seedbed for raising plants

A seedbed from which plants will be transplanted must be in an open position, not in an out-of-the-way and perhaps shaded corner where seedlings may become drawn. Clean the ground as thoroughly as possible of annual and perennial weeds. The rows in a seedbed can be relatively close together, say 8 inches for brassicas (20 cm), but sowing *in* the rows must be as thinly as when sowing direct in drills, to about 1½ inches (3 cm) apart, otherwise plant roots become overcrowded and entangled, and are damaged when lifted.

Sowing in a drill

This is the commonest method of sowing outdoors. Prepare the seedbed as above, then mark the position of the row with a line, making a drill along the line, using the point of a trowel or the corner of a draw hoe. The depth of the drill depends on the size of the seed, but it is important to keep the depth uniform, otherwise germination will be uneven, with seeds sown more deeply emerging more slowly. Very large seeds like beans need to be $1\frac{1}{2}$ to 2 inches deep (38–50 mm), peas and sweet corn 1 to $1\frac{1}{2}$ inches deep (25–38 mm), brassicas $\frac{3}{4}$ to 1 inch (20–25 mm) and small seeds like carrots, leeks, lettuces and onions $\frac{1}{2}$ to $\frac{3}{4}$ inch (12–20 mm) deep. If the soil is dry water the drill before sowing.

Seed is sown along the drill *as thinly as possible*, to reduce the need for thinning. If sown too thickly, the overcrowded seedlings will be poor specimens, with little chance of producing a quality crop. With practice small seeds from a pinch held between thumb and forefinger can be dropped singly into the drill. Small seeds can be sown more evenly if they are mixed with sand. Pelleted seeds (see p. 20) can easily be sown at the spacing required.

Seeds can either be spaced evenly along the row or sown in groups of three to four seeds at intervals a few inches apart. Where plants will eventually be thinned to 10 inches apart (25 cm), they can be sown initially at positions 5 inches apart (12 cm).

Finally cover the seed with soil using a rake, a trowel or by hand. If birds are a problem put one or two strands of strong black cotton along the drill, about 2 inches above the soil (5 cm) immediately after sowing, to protect the emerging seedlings.

Sowing large seeds

Very large seeds such as pumpkins, marrows, sweet corn, beans can be sown by making a small hole with a dibber. Place the seed carefully in the hole, making sure it has reached the bottom, and cover with soil. Jam jars can be put over the seed to keep the soil moist and so encourage germination. Sow a few 'spares' for transplanting into any gaps caused by germination failures, or sow several seeds per station, thinning to one per site after germination.

Covering seedbeds

One of the most common causes of seeds failing to germinate is soil drying out. This can be prevented by covering the seedbed or drills with newspaper, ordinary or slitted plastic film or even light straw until the seed has germinated. The plastic can be anchored by burying the edge in the soil. Any covering, except slitted plastic, must be removed as soon as any seedlings are visible, or they become drawn. Watering the soil after sowing is a bad practice as the fine top layer is likely to 'cap', and seedlings find it difficult to emerge through this.

Sowing in adverse conditions

Sowing in cold and wet conditions is inadvisable, but where it is unavoidable, work from a wooden board placed on the ground, to avoid compacting the soil. A drill can be opened up and covered with cloches for a few days, to warm and dry out the soil; alternatively a little peat or sowing or potting compost can be put in the bottom of the drill before sowing. This will absorb moisture from the soil and help the seed to germinate.

Sowing in dry conditions

This situation is most likely to occur with late spring or summer sowings. Take out the drill and water the bottom of it with a small-spouted can. Then sow the seed and cover it with *dry* soil. The dry soil acts as a mulch, so preventing evaporation, and enabling the seed to germinate.

Fluid sowing

Seeds of several vegetables (e.g. beetroot, carrots and parsnips) need a higher temperature for germination than for subsequent growth of seedlings. In a cold spring the soil will be slow to warm up and seeds of these crops sown into a cold soil will not germinate. A new technique called fluid sowing shows promise of overcoming this. Seeds are germinated indoors in favourable conditions, and the seedlings, which will develop in slightly cooler soil conditions than the seeds, are then sown outside.

Seeds are germinated a few days before sowing outdoors, the interval depending on the crop. Lettuces, for instance, will germinate in a day at room temperature, but celery may take 10 days to reach 50% germination. The seeds are sown on damp absorbent paper and kept at about 70 °F (21 °C). The seedlings are ready for sowing when the young roots are no longer than $\frac{1}{5}$ inch (5 mm). These young plants are mixed with a gel (made up of e.g. diluted non-fungicidal wallpaper paste) which acts as a carrier. The gel with the seedlings is put into a flexible container (plastic bag or bottle) and expelled along the seed drill. The drill is covered in as with conventional sowing.

As well as improving the emergence of seedlings, fluid sowing makes it easier to spread out the seeds (especially small seeds) in the drills, and with practice there is no need for thinning later. (Details of the technique are given in the leaflet *Fluid sowing* available from the National Vegetable Research Station.)

FLUID SOWING

1 *Sowing from the packet on to moistened paper.*

2 *The seeds have just started to germinate and are ready to be transferred to the gel.*

3 *Washing the seeds off the paper.*

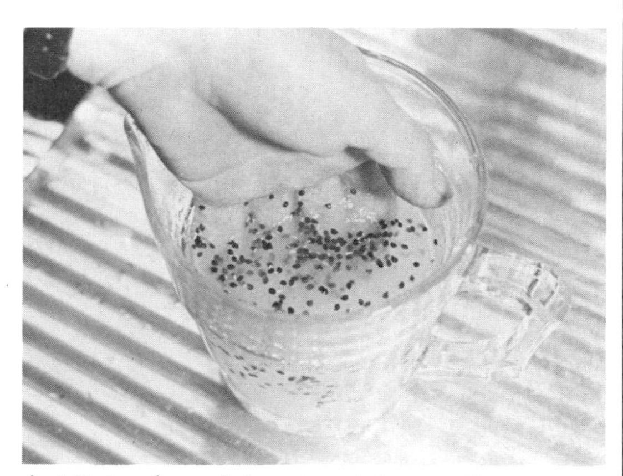

4 *Mixing the seeds into the gel for easy flow.*

5 *The seed/gel mixture in a plastic bag, the end cut off just before sowing.*

6 *Sowing the mixture with seedlings into a seed drill.*

Photographs reproduced by permission of the National Vegetable Research Station.

Broadcasting

Seed is scattered thinly on to a moist, well-prepared seedbed as thinly and evenly as possible. The seed is raked into the soil first in one direction, then at right angles to the first raking, or is covered by riddling soil over the seed.

Broadcasting makes good use of the cropping area, but because of the uneven distribution of the crop plants it is difficult to weed. Make sure the ground is clean before sowing; if there is time prepare the seedbed, allow the first flush of weeds to germinate and hoe them off before sowing.

Broadcasting is used for growing patches of crops such as early carrots, mustard and cress, and turnip greens. It is also recommended for cut-and-come-again crops. This productive technique utilizes the fact that many leafy vegetables will re-sprout several times when cut an inch or so above ground level at stages varying from a large seedling to a mature plant. Lettuce, leaf chicories, salad rocket, parsley and spinach are among suitable crops for this.

Intersowing

To make good use of space two different crops can be sown in one drill, for example slow growing parsnips with fast growing radishes or small cultivars of lettuce. The radishes or lettuce will emerge earlier, indicating where the rows are (which makes early hoeing easier); they will mature long before their space is needed by the parsnips.

INTERSOWING

Parsnips intersown with lettuces.

Thinning

With careful sowing, thinning should not be necessary. If it is, try to minimize the disturbance to neighbouring plants. The final distance to which seedlings are thinned depends on the crop.

Thin as soon as the seedlings are large enough to handle. Always thin when the ground is moist to minimize root disturbance, watering beforehand if necessary. Firm the soil around the base of the remaining plants and remove thinnings, which may attract pests.

Root disturbance can be kept to a minimum by nipping off the surplus seedlings at soil level, leaving the roots behind, rather than pulling up the whole plant. This method has the additional advantage that it can be done when the soil is dry.

SOWING INDOORS

By sowing in protected conditions indoors, higher rates of germination can be achieved than by outdoor sowings. Plants can also be started indoors when conditions outdoors are still unsuitable for sowing. 'Indoors' means in a house, greenhouse, frame or even under cloches.

Sowing composts

Various mixtures are sold for plant raising. They are based either on peat or soil, the former being lighter to use but more liable to dry out. Seed is sown in sowing compost, and seedlings and young plants moved on into potting compost, which is coarser and enriched with more fertilizer. Compost adequate for the early stages of plant growth can be made by mixing two parts of sand with one part of peat or leaf mould and one part of sieved loam.

Sowing

Seed boxes or pots are loosely filled with well-moistened compost, striking off the top with a stick to get level filling. Then the compost is pressed firmly with a board to give a ½ inch space (1 cm) at the top of the container. Seeds are sown thinly on the level surface and are covered by sieving a little compost over them, finally pressing the surface level with the board. If the compost was well moistened no further watering will be necessary. If the surface is dry, stand the container in a basin of water to soak up moisture, but not so deep that the water flows over the top of the box and dislodges the seeds.

To maintain a moist atmosphere, and so encourage germination, cover the seed box with

SOWING INDOORS

1 *After filling the tray with compost and firming it the top is levelled off.*

2 *The seeds are sown thinly on the surface.*

3 *Pressing the seeds into the compost.*

4 *A thin layer of fine compost is sieved over the seeds.*

SOWING INDOORS

Seeds can also be sown in pots.

newspaper and a sheet of glass or plastic film after sowing: some seed trays have a plastic dome incorporated which serves the same purpose. Remove the covering for about half an hour a day for ventilation, and remove it altogether as soon as the seed has germinated.

Seeds need warmth to germinate, the minimum temperature varying with the crop. Germination is fastest with 'bottom heat', i.e. a source of heat from below, such as in an electric propagator.

Once seeds have germinated they must be moved into a good light, though they will need to be shaded from very bright sunlight in the early stages. Do not allow the compost to dry out.

Pricking out

As soon as seedlings are becoming crowded in their original container they must be transferred to a bigger container or individual pots, allowing them space to develop. This is known as pricking out.

Water the seedlings, then fill the bigger tray or pots with moist compost. Using a small dibber, old kitchen fork or miniature trowel, lift each seedling and separate it carefully from its neighbours, holding it by a leaf. Make a small hole in the compost just large enough for the roots, and press the seedling gently but firmly into the hole, so that the lowest leaves are just above soil level. Shade the seedlings from bright sunlight until they have started growing again. They can normally remain in these containers until conditions are suitable for planting outdoors.

Seedlings can also be sown spaciously in a seed tray, each several inches apart, so avoiding pricking out. The disadvantage of this is that more heated space is required in the earlier stages.

Sowing in blocks

Pricking out can also be avoided by sowing seeds in cubes of soil or compost known as 'blocks'. This is a useful method of raising vegetables, especially where only limited numbers of plants are required.

The seedlings develop an excellent root system in the block, and when ready the block is planted out whole, so minimizing disturbance to the plant at any stage.

Blocking compost is the most suitable medium, but ordinary soil or peat-based potting compost can be used although it holds together less satisfactorily. Blocks of approximately $1\frac{1}{2}$ inch cube ($3\,cm^3$) with a small hole in the upper surface are made with hand blocking tools. The blocks are placed, almost touching, on a board or in a seed tray.

One to three seeds are sown by hand in the hole in each block, usually thinning to one per block after germination. Seeds too small to be handled easily can be pushed carefully off a piece of board or glass, or lifted individually on the point of a small damp (watercolour) paint brush. They will adhere to the brush and drop off when touched on to the block. The seed is covered with soil from the edge of the hole, and then left to germinate as when sown in boxes.

Hardening off

Whatever system is used for raising plants indoors, before planting out they must be acclimatized, or hardened off, over a ten to fourteen day period. If the plants are in frames or under cloches these should be ventilated or removed for increasingly longer periods each day. If in a greenhouse they can be moved into frames or cloches as an intermediate stage, or moved outdoors, first for a few hours during the day, then for longer periods. Hardening off is particularly important for plants raised in peat-based, rather than soil-based composts. The former encourage softer growth which is more susceptible to cold.

PRICKING OUT

1 *Smoothing the surface of the potting compost.*

2 *Celery seedlings are being pricked out in a seed tray.*

SOWING IN BLOCKS

1 *Making peat blocks with a special hand tool.*

2 *The seeds are sown into the hole on the top of the block.*

Planting

The moment to plant is determined by soil and weather conditions, and the state of the plant itself. Planting represents a check to the plant, and everything should be done to minimize the check so that plants become established rapidly. For this reason planting in wet and/or cold soil and in adverse weather conditions is never advisable. Half-hardy plants cannot be planted outside until the risk of hard frost is over, which varies from early May in the south of England to early or mid June in colder parts of the country.

Within reason, the younger a plant is transplanted the better. Lettuces can be planted at the 4 to 6 leaf stage; brassicas when they are about 4 inches high (10 cm). Transplanting root crops is not very satisfactory except when they are very small. This does not apply to block- and pot-raised plants, which, provided they have not become starved, can be planted successfully at almost any stage.

Planting

The ground is prepared in advance by forking (except when planting brassicas), removing weeds, and raking over the surface. A fine tilth is unnecessary and undesirable as it encourages weed-seed germination, but a relatively level surface makes planting easier. Ideally the soil should be moist. It is best to plant in the evening or when conditions are overcast, so that the plant is not put immediately into conditions that may lead to wilting.

Whether the plants are in a seedbed, pots, boxes or blocks, they must be well watered several hours before planting. This has been shown to be far more important than watering after they are planted – although in some cases both are necessary.

Transplanting from blocks gives less disturbance. Make sure that the block is well watered *before* transplanting.

Lift the individual plants carefully using a trowel, holding them by the leaves or stems rather than the roots, as the root hairs are easily damaged. Using a trowel, make a hole in the soil large enough to accommodate the roots easily. Hold the plant in place with one hand, and fill the soil in around the roots. Finally firm the soil around the stem; tug a leaf to make sure the plant is not loose.

Where the ground is dry, water around the base of the plant after planting. Mulching (see p. 38) at the same time will help to conserve the moisture. In very hot weather shade the plants from strong sun for the first few days until they become established. An upturned pot over the plant will do and it can also be done with cones of newspaper.

For plants that will eventually require staking (e.g. runner beans) it is best to put in the stake just before planting or sowing.

Heeling in

When plants have been bought in, but weather conditions make immediate planting impossible, heel them in for up to a week as an emergency measure, to prevent the roots from drying out. This can be done by making a small V-shaped slit a few inches deep in the soil. The plants are disentangled and laid singly but close together in the slit, the roots at the bottom, and the stems against one side of the V. The roots and lower parts of the stem are then covered with moist soil, so that all roots are in contact with the soil.

Occasionally it is necessary to lift the last of a crop, parsnips or leeks for example, at the end of their season (March/April) when the ground is needed for the next crop. The plants can be heeled in similarly until required for use. They will keep in a reasonable condition for several weeks.

Spacing

As discussed in the introduction, the traditional method of growing vegetables in rows with relatively wide spaces between the rows is now being challenged by the concept of growing plants at equidistant spacing in narrow beds. Where planting in rows is still practised, closer plantings than previously are being adopted and it is recommended that plants *in* the adjacent rows should be staggered. Whatever system is used, it is important to allow each individual plant enough space in each direction to grow to its optimum size.

Research has also been done on the relations between spacing and vegetable size, so that in many cases spacing can now be used as a tool to determine the size of the vegetable you want. To take an example: onions can be sown ½ inch (1 cm) apart in 12 inch rows (30 cm) to get pickling onions, 1 inch by 4 inches (2.5 × 10 cm) for spring onions, and 1½ inches (3.5 cm) apart in 12 inch rows (30 cm) to obtain large cooking onions. With summer cabbage the highest yields of small heads is obtained by planting 14 inches by 14 inches (35 × 35 cm); larger cabbages are produced by planting at 18 inches by 18 inches (45 × 45 cm). So where a family requires

PLANTING

1 *Watering the seedlings in the seedbed before lifting them.*

2 *Firming in a brassica plant, showing the correct depth of planting.*

3 *Planting leeks into a hole. For this crop, the hole does not need to be filled in.*

4 *Planting lettuces using a trowel, using traditional spacing, 9 × 9 inches apart.*

only moderate-sized summer cabbages the former spacing is advisable, but where extra large cabbages are required, a more generous spacing can be adopted. With cabbages this would give slightly earlier yields – though earliness and sparser planting do not necessarily go hand in hand. Further examples will be mentioned where appropriate.

Intercropping
Just as two crops can sometimes be sown within a row to save space, different crops can be intercropped, i.e. one sown or planted between rows of another. For example young brassica plants can be planted between rows of early peas. They will not spread into the area occupied by the peas until later in the season, when the peas have been cleared. Quick-maturing crops such as radishes, turnips, early carrots, small varieties of lettuce are useful for growing between rows of longer growing crops.

Wherever intercropping is practised, care must be taken to allow enough space, light and moisture for each crop to develop. It is important to remember that competition from weeds or another crop can affect yields. There must also be enough room for access for cultivation and picking. For these reasons it may be advisable to have rows a little further apart than usual where intercropping is planned. It is best to avoid intercropping naturally sprawling vegetables such as potatoes, which tend to engulf smaller plants in their vicinity. But marrows and dwarf beans, for example, can be grown successfully beneath sweet corn.

INTERCROPPING

Lettuce rows interplanted with brassicas.

Water and Watering

Vegetables only grow well when they have a sufficient supply of water, which is taken in through their roots and evaporated from their leaves. This constant uptake of water keeps the stomata on the leaves open and the plant turgid, enabling respiration, photosynthesis, and the absorption and use of nutrients to take place at maximum efficiency. Growth is reduced if for any reason there is a shortage of water.

The soil is the plant's reservoir of water. When, after free drainage has taken place, the soil is holding as much water as it can, it is said to be at *field capacity*; when there is so little water in the soil that roots can no longer extract it and plants wilt, it is at the *permanent wilting point*. Between these extremes water in the soil is *available* to plants.

Soils vary tremendously in the amount of available water they can hold, depending on their texture and structure. The better the structure, the more water it can hold and the longer it can sustain plants without recourse to supplementary watering. Soils with the largest particles – the coarse-textured soils such as light sandy soils – have the poorest water holding capacity; those with a good proportion of all particle sizes – the medium-textured soils, such as silty loams – are the best for retaining available water.

Water is mainly lost from the upper layers of the soil, through evaporation from both the soil surface and plant leaves. Sunshine, temperature, wind, relative humidity and the amount of moisture in the soil surface all affect the rate of evaporation. Evaporation is greatest in dry sunny windy weather, from a moist surface. Once the top few inches of soil have dried out evaporation is very much reduced – a fact which has important implications for water conservation in the soil.

Another fundamental fact is that the soil becomes wet layer by layer. Until the top layer is saturated, the soil beneath remains dry. Water will only reach a point say 6 inches down (15 cm) when all the soil above is saturated. So watering lightly on the surface is quite ineffective; watering has to be thorough if water is to reach the lower parts of the root zone.

Measures for reducing watering
It is a waste of time and resources to over water and much can be done to minimize the need for water, by taking various measures to conserve the water in the soil.

WATERING

1 *A revolving-type nozzle watering a circular area.*

2 *A square-area sprinkler in action.*

Improving the soil structure. Working well-rotted bulky organic matter such as farmyard manure or compost into the soil regularly, mixed thoroughly over the whole depth of rooting, increases the water-holding capacity of most soils (see p. 6).

Mulching prevents evaporation from the soil. It is best done after watering or after rain.

Deep digging encourages roots to grow to greater depths, so drawing water from deeper reserves.

Shallow cultivation. In dry weather cultivation should be restricted to surface hoeing, done only to remove weeds. Deeper cultivation brings moist soil to the surface, from which water is lost by evaporation.

Weeding. Established weeds compete for water and contribute to water loss from the soil through transpiration. Aim to remove them as seedlings.

Sparse planting. Wider spacing enables each plant to draw water from a larger volume of soil, and it can be adopted if space is not limited – especially on light soils.

Shelter. Windbreaks help to cut down water loss through evaporation. Living windbreaks such as hedges, however, compete for water in the soil.

When to water

In a normal year winter rains bring the soil to field capacity at the start of the vegetable sowing season. Water is lost throughout the summer by evaporation, unless natural rainfall replenishes the supply. In most summers *adequate* yields can be obtained without extra watering. However, for optimum yields the plants need ample water (and nutrients) applied at the right time, so supplementary watering is necessary.

In general, watering encourages leaf growth; so it is most directly beneficial for plants with edible foliage such as brassicas, lettuces and spinach.

Too much water may in some cases be counter-productive. It can increase plant growth without increasing the edible part; with root crops, for example, excess water may encourage lush leaf

3 *Layflat tubing, which waters the root area directly.*

growth without a corresponding response from the roots. Excess water also discourages roots from penetrating the soil, making plants more susceptible to drought; it may leach nitrogenous fertilizers away from the root zone; and it may reduce the flavour.

With root crops, such as carrots and parsnips, watering after a dry spell can cause the roots to swell so rapidly that they split. Watering bulb onions in the later stages of growth can delay ripening.

However, if for any reason the soil becomes dry or root growth is restricted, watering is beneficial. But it is important to understand the effect of watering at different stages of development on different parts of the plant.

Many plants go through stages in their development when the supply of water is critical. These are moisture-sensitive periods. Examples are peas when flowers and pods are forming and maincrop potatoes when tubers are at the marble size. Watering at these sensitive stages increases yields; when water is scarce concentrate its application at these times.

The art of watering effectively, especially where water, or time to water, is scarce, is embodied in three principles: limiting amounts, limiting frequency, and concentrating on moisture-sensitive and other critical periods.

Limiting amounts and frequency. A few heavy waterings give the best returns on time and effort. In hot weather it is generally not worth giving less than 2 gal./sq. yd (11 litres/m^2) at any one time. Directing water at the base of the plant, leaving the surrounding area dry, is the most economical way of watering. Where this 'point watering' is adopted, however, watering needs to be more frequent than when the whole area is watered. Frequency and quantity need to be varied according to the soil. Light soils need to be watered more frequently than heavy, moisture-retentive soils, but with smaller quantities of water at each watering.

Although heavy watering is recommended, big *droplets*, applied overhead, can damage the soil surface and seedlings. The gentler the watering, the smaller the drops of water, the better.

Critical periods

Establishing seeds and seedlings. Seeds will not germinate nor seedlings become established if there is insufficient water in the soil. Where the ground is very dry in spring, water the seedbed a couple of days in advance of sowing. This gives time for the surface to dry out sufficiently to be raked to a tilth before sowing. An alternative is to water individual drills with about 1 gal. of water to 20 feet (1 litre to 1.3 m). Where seedlings must be watered use a light rose with the spray directed upwards, so that a shower of small droplets is produced.

Transplanting. If the soil is not moist at planting, water each transplant, confining the water to a circle about 6 inches diameter (15 cm) around the plant stem. As roots tend to be damaged by transplanting, this is one case where watering little but often is the rule until the plants become established. In dry weather daily watering with $\frac{1}{4}$ pint (140 ml) to each plant is recommended.

Leafy crops

For most leafy crops (brassicas, lettuces, spinach, celery), frequent watering results in heavy yields and succulent crops. In the dry months of summer they will benefit from 2 to 3 gal./sq. yd/week (11–16 litres/m^2). Where this is impossible, confine watering to a heavy application of about 4 gal./sq. yd (22 litres/m²) from 10 to 20 days before maturity. Brussels sprouts are an exception: they are generally so widely spaced that no extra watering is normally required.

'Fruiting' vegetables

The critical periods with vegetables where the seeds and fruits are eaten – tomatoes, cucumbers, marrows, sweet corn, peas and beans – are at flowering time and when fruits are setting and swelling. Water generously at these stages, giving up to 4 gal./sq. yd per week (22 litres/m²). Watering in the period after establishment and before flowering is only necessary if the plants show signs of wilting. Excess watering during this period induces too much leaf growth.

Root crops

With most root crops such as carrot, beetroot, radish, parsnip, the aim is to apply enough water to maintain steady growth without encouraging lush foliage. In the early stages 1 gal./yd of row (5 litres/m of row) is sufficient in dry weather; but when the storage roots are actively growing, 3 to 4 gal./sq. yd (16–22 litres/m²) every fortnight may be necessary. At no stage should the soil be allowed to dry out. (For potato watering see p. 119.)

Watering equipment

For watering in small gardens a watering can is quite adequate, with a fine rose for watering small plants. For larger gardens there are various types of automatic sprinklers on the market, which can be connected to the mains supply with a garden hose. These wet fairly large areas of ground but need to be moved frequently. Distribution of water is sometimes uneven, particularly with rotary sprinklers which water a circular area, resulting in overlapping and unwatered areas.

A useful type of automatic system is the thin-walled 'layflat' polythene tubing, perforated with holes about 12 inches apart (30 cm). This can be laid alongside rows of plants so that a strip about 12 inches wide (30 cm) is watered. The tubing can either be connected to a hose pipe, or run from a water supply in a tank or water barrow at very low pressure. The water seeps gently through the tubing around the plants roots. A great advantage of lay-flat tubing is that it is easily moved. It is also suitable for use in a greenhouse.

Weeds

Weeds in vegetable gardens compete with the crop for water, nutrients and light. Moreover, many common weeds are closely related botanically to many common vegetables, and may harbour serious pests and diseases, sometimes providing a host for these during the winter.

There are two classes of weeds. Perennials, generally characterized by invasive spreading stems or roots or very deep tap roots, persist in the soil from one year to the next. Ground elder, field bindweed, dock, dandelion, couch grass, creeping thistle and horsetail are some of the worst. Annuals germinate, flower and die in one season, and may even complete several cycles in a year. Chickweed, groundsel, annual meadow grass are typical of these.

Annuals

There are thousands of viable seeds of annual weeds in the top few inches of soil. Some (groundsel, chickweed) are relatively short-lived; others (fat hen, fool's parsley) can remain dormant in the soil for decades. When soil is regularly cultivated about 50% of these seeds are lost each year through germinating on the surface, germinating under the soil and failing to emerge, or through exposure to birds, climate, weathering and so on. It takes the proverbial seven years ('one year's seeding is seven years' weeding') to reduce the seed reserves in cultivated soil to about 1% of the original level. Regular cultivation, therefore, helps to keep down weeds. It is particularly important to prevent weeds going to seed: a single plant of fat hen has produced as many as 70,000 seeds.

In uncultivated ground far fewer seeds are lost annually. So when such ground *is* cultivated there is a huge flush of weeds. The best way to deal with this is to cultivate the ground, allow the first flush to germinate, and then hoe off these weeds before sowing or planting. Shallow cultivation is advisable in the early stages to prevent more seeds being brought up from lower levels.

Research has shown that the weeds which offer the most serious competition to growing vegetables are those *between* rather than within the rows. So weeding between the rows is always beneficial, even if there is not time to weed in the rows. In general competition from weeds begins to become serious about 3 weeks after a vegetable crop has germinated, so efforts should be concentrated on removing weeds by this time. Start weeding as soon as the crop row can be seen.

HOEING

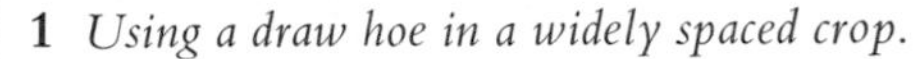

1 *Using a draw hoe in a widely spaced crop.*

2 *With an onion hoe, closer weeding can be done.*

Crops with broad and spreading leaves such as beet, brassicas, and carrots will naturally smother much weed growth by forming a canopy over the soil. Equidistant spacing would allow fairly quick establishment of the canopy, but in practice growing in rows allows easier weed control in the earlier stages by hoeing. Crops with narrow leaves such as onions have no smothering effect, and if they cannot be hand weeded, it is better to grow them in rows far enough apart to allow for hoeing.

Hoeing and hand weeding are the most practical methods of controlling annual weeds in a vegetable garden. Hoeing should be as shallow as possible to minimize damage to plant roots, and to prevent more weed seed being brought up to the surface. It is best to hoe in dry weather, while weeds are still small. They can then be left on the soil surface to die. Larger weeds left on the surface in wet weather may re-root.

Perennials

These must be recognized and are best removed when ground is dug over in the winter, taking care to remove even small pieces of root, or rhizome, which will re-sprout. Many are liable to re-sprout if the tops are merely hoed off, hence the importance of digging them out completely.

Chemical weed control

The most useful of the chemical weedkillers in the vegetable garden are the 'site clearance' types, e.g. paraquat/diquat mixture and glyphosate. They can also be applied between growing crops, but this needs to be done with extreme care. Both materials kill any green tissue they touch so are safest to use when no crop is present. Neither leave residues in the soil after application.

The soil-acting weedkillers need very careful and regulated application to avoid any build-up of residues in the soil or damage to crops. They control germinating annual weeds when applied to weed-free soil. Propachlor is effective for several weeks and is useful in seedbeds of onions, leeks and brassicas, and after transplanting. Propham/chlorpropham mixture can be used with newly transplanted and established plants. Simazine controls germinating weed seedlings for several months and can be used round asparagus and rhubarb but cannot be recommended among other vegetables.

At present, therefore, the use of herbicides among vegetables is limited, and weeds are more effectively controlled by early hoeing, mulching and by closer spacing of the rows so that the crop grows quickly over the inter-row spaces and smothers the weeds.

Mulching

Mulching is the practice of covering the soil surface with a layer of protective material. This is usually of an organic nature, such as compost or straw, which will rot down, but plastic mulches are becoming more widely used.

Mulching has a number of beneficial effects:

It helps to conserve soil moisture by slowing down its evaporation.

It helps to prevent weed-seed germination.

It improves soil structure, by mitigating the effects of treading on soil, and by encouraging earthworm activity.

It helps plant roots to extract nutrients by keeping the upper layers of the soil moist.

When used under trailing crops such as bush tomatoes, marrows or cucumbers it helps to keep the fruit clean and dry.

It can protect crops being overwintered in the soil, preserving the soil structure and enabling them to be lifted more easily in severe frost.

MULCHING

Runner beans in particular benefit from a good mulch to help conserve moisture.

Organic mulches

What to use for mulching is largely governed by what is available. Organic mulches increase the organic matter in the soil. They can either be dug in at the end of the season, or left on the surface for the worms to work in. The ideal material is well rotted (so that nitrogen is not taken from the soil in the early stages of its decomposition), does not form too solid and impermeable a layer which prevents rain from penetrating, and is pleasant to handle. The thickness of the mulch depends on the material used, but it can be between $1\frac{1}{2}$ and 4 inches thick (4–10 cm).

The following are suitable materials: garden compost, spent mushroom compost, rotted animal manures, straw (especially short straw), seaweed, pine needles, leaf mould, lawn mowings, peat, rotted sawdust, wood shavings, shredded and pulverized bark. Some of these materials have disadvantages.

Garden compost, if poorly made, is likely to contain weed seeds (see pp. 12–14).

Seaweed may attract flies, but can be covered with a sprinkling of soil to deter them.

Wood derivatives such as sawdust, wood shavings, shredded and pulverized bark, and pine needles should be used in moderation on cultivated ground and among growing crops, because while decomposing they use the nitrogen in the soil, so depriving the plants of nitrogen.

Peat should not be used in too thick a layer as initially it will absorb most of the rainfall before it filters through to the soil.

Plastic mulches

Various types of plastic film are available. They can either be held in place by weighting the ends and edges, or, more satisfactorily, by burying the edges into a slit in the soil made with a trowel. If handled carefully they can be used several times. *Black film* is used primarily for weed control, especially for potatoes, eliminating the need for earthing up. It is laid over the ground when the tubers are planted, and holes are cut in the plastic as the plants start to push it up. Seeds of such plants as sweet corn can also be sown through black plastic, by punching holes in the plastic with a dibber or a knife and sowing through the holes. They can also be transplanted through the slits.

Individual plants such as marrows and pumpkins benefit by being mulched with plastic after planting. The plastic can be unrolled along the rows, cutting crossed slits in the plastic above the plant, through which the leaves are eased.

Slugs enjoy the conditions under black plastic; so scatter some slug pellets over the soil surface before covering it with plastic. Before laying slope the ground slightly towards the plants so that the rain drains towards them.

Clear film is particularly useful for helping to warm up the soil in spring before sowing, and for mulching seedbeds, conserving surface moisture until the seeds have germinated. It must be removed as soon as the seedlings can be seen. The more recently introduced perforated clear films expand with the plants, so can be left in place for several weeks to several months, depending on the crop.

How and when to mulch

Mulching tends to maintain the current status of the soil, so avoid mulching when the soil is cold, dry, or *very* wet. The ideal is to mulch when the soil is moist but warm.

It is often convenient to mulch after planting. When seeds are sown direct in the soil, mulch between the rows once the seedlings are clearly visible. This is a good time for the first hoeing, and the mulch can be applied immediately after.

Crops such as peas, beans, carrots and sweet corn can be mulched between the plants or between rows once they are well established.

Overwintering crops such as celeriac, leeks, parsnips, winter radishes can be mulched with straw or dried bracken in the autumn. This is primarily for crop protection, but also to make it easier to lift the roots in frosty weather.

Shelter

Research has shown that with almost all vegetables shelter from even light winds can increase yields by up to 20 to 30%. Protection from strong winds will give even greater increases. Shelter is particularly valuable in winter when temperatures are low, for it is the combination of low temperature and strong wind which does serious damage to plants. In coastal areas windbreaks provide valuable protection against salt spray.

The best windbreak is about 50% permeable, so that the wind is filtered through it. When wind encounters a solid barrier it is forced over it, creating a very destructive area of turbulence on the far side. Generally speaking, a windbreak is effective for a distance of from six to ten times its height, providing less and less shelter the further one is from it. So for maximum effect, erect barriers about 3 feet high (1 m) at 18 ft apart (6 m).

Windbreaks fall into two categories: living and artificial. One of the most effective artificial fences is a lath screen, constructed by nailing horizontal lath strips an inch wide (2.5 cm), an inch apart, on to a lath framework.

There are many manufactured net and web materials on the market for use as windbreaks. These are attached to stakes with battens. In strong wind fences and nets must take tremendous strain so need to be very securely erected. Stakes used should be sturdy (at least 2 to 3 inches (5–7.5 cm) diameter), and rot proof. They should be erected at about 6 feet apart (1.8 m) for netting; and 10 feet (3 m) for wooden lath fences.

Around the circumference of a garden artificial windbreaks normally need to be at least 6 feet high (1.8 m), which represents a fairly expensive investment. Where this is impossible smaller windbreaks, rather on the style of tennis nets, can be erected between rows of plants to give very valuable protection. These need be no more than 1½ feet high (45 cm). Home-made windbreaks of this type can be made from material such as hessian. Even ½ inch mesh wire netting (2 cm) has some effect as a windbreak, breaking the force of severe winds and mitigating hail damage.

Trees and hedges offer the most permanent windbreaks, but take several years to become effective, require maintenance, compete for water and nutrients, and may create shade. On a smaller scale, tall growing crops such as sweet corn, jerusalem artichokes and sunflowers can serve as temporary living windbreaks.

SHELTER

A shelter screen of netting erected to protect outdoor tomato plants.

Severe wind damage can be caused by draughts and 'wind funnels', often created by gaps between buildings. It is worth erecting windbreaks across such gaps, to stretch a couple of feet beyond the gap on either side. Where shrubs are planted in gaps as windbreaks, artificial protection may be necessary until they are established.

Although shelter is invaluable, plants should never be grown in totally sheltered, still conditions as these encourage a rapid build up of pests and diseases.

Vegetable Storage

Wherever possible vegetables should be used fresh: once they are picked they start to deteriorate, because of water loss, and to lose flavour. Any method of storing the surplus crop must aim to keep the rate of water loss at its lowest.

Deep freezing (although not strictly storage, but preservation) has made a great difference to vegetable storage, and there are plenty of specialist books giving details of methods.

Root crops

Many root crops (parsnips, swedes and carrots) are frost tolerant and can often be 'stored' in the soil instead of being lifted, particularly if grown on light well-drained soils. The advantage of leaving them in the soil is that there is considerably less water loss than when they are lifted. The disadvantages are the risk of slug and other pest damage (worst on heavy soils) and the unpleasantness and difficulty of lifting in wet and cold weather.

Where vegetables are left in the ground mark the ends of the rows so they can be found in snow, and cover them when soil temperatures have fallen to their winter level of about 41 °F (5 °C), with a thick layer of straw or bracken, held in place with wire hoops if necessary. This is about mid to late November in the south and end October to early November in the north. This layer will give protection from severe frost and make it possible to dig the soil to lift the roots even during frosty weather.

Most root vegetables can be conveniently stored in boxes, barrels or bins in layers of slightly moist sand or peat. The advantage is that they are easy to get at when needed but the moisture loss is relatively rapid. Handle roots for storage very gently, rub off surplus mud and trim or twist off leaves. Reject diseased and damaged roots or store them separately and use them first.

Place the largest roots at the bottom of the container so that smaller roots, which lose moisture faster, are used first. Cover the top layer so that no roots are exposed. Keep the containers in a frost-proof building such as a cellar, or soundly built shed, where temperatures are as close to a uniform 32 °F (0 °C) as possible, and mice are not likely to be a problem.

Potatoes are susceptible to frost damage, and cannot be left in the ground. Store them at temperatures between 39° and 50 °F (4 and 10 °C). Give them extra protection if the temperature is

STORAGE OF ROOTS

1 *Beetroot stored in sand in a box.*

2 *Starting a swede clamp, by placing the roots on a layer of straw.*

likely to fall any lower. They are best stored in tomato trays, so that they get enough ventilation, covered with old carpet or sacks to keep out the light. Double-thickness paper sacks tied at the neck may also be used, but should not be filled too full. Potatoes must be stored away from light, which stimulates the formation of poisonous alkaloids in tubers. Plastic sacks are not suitable as the conditions in them become too humid.

The traditional method of storing root vegetables is in clamps, which can either be made outdoors, or on the floor in outbuildings or cellars. Vegetables in clamps are easier to get at than when left in the open ground, but there may be a fairly high wastage of roots. Clamps are used much less today, but swedes, carrots, turnips, potatoes are among the vegetables that can be stored in this way.

Clamps should be made on well-drained ground. They are sometimes made against a wall, and can be round, semicircular or oblong. Roots are piled up in a neat heap as high as required (except for carrots which should not be piled more than 2 feet high (60 cm)) on a layer of straw about 8 inches thick (20 cm). The top of the heap is covered with another layer of straw of about the same thickness, and then a layer of earth about 6 inches thick (15 cm). This is taken from around the outside of the clamp, so making a small drainage ditch around it. For very hardy roots such as swedes the final layer of earth is unnecessary. A watch should be kept for mice and rats which may burrow into clamps.

Leafy vegetables

Spinach, lettuce, spring cabbage, brussels sprouts, and sprouting vegetables such as broccoli and cauliflower lose moisture very rapidly once picked, and are difficult to store for any length of time. They are well suited to deep freezing.

To maximize their short-term storage life they are best picked early or late in the day, when at their coolest, further cooled as quickly as possible by being put in a refrigerator or cool shed (not in plastic bags) or plunged in cold water and shaken dry, then kept in a refrigerator in a plastic bag with the top folded over to restrict ventilation.

Certain hearted vegetables such as winter cabbages (and to some extent summer cabbages), hearted Sugar Loaf chicories and endive and Chinese cabbage can be stored in various ways for periods ranging from several weeks to several months. Temperatures should be as near 32 °F (0 °C) as possible, and the atmosphere fairly moist. Tolerance to frost varies, but they can generally be kept in a frost-free shed or cellar, either on racks or shelves or hung in nets. The hardiest types of cabbages can be stored outside in cold frames, placed on wooden slats to keep them off the ground. The frames are covered with matting or sacks in severe weather, and opened for ventilation on sunny winter days.

Inspect stored cabbages and other leafy vegetables regularly, gently rolling off any diseased or withered outer leaves with the palm of the hand.

Onions, shallots and garlic

These are best stored in frost-free conditions but at low temperatures, ideally 32 °F (0 °C), with as much ventilation as possible. Good harvesting is the key to good storage and this is greatly helped if it can be done during dry weather. As soon as the foliage has died down ease the bulbs gently out of the ground, and spread them to dry on sacks, trays or netting raised off the ground outdoors. In a period of prolonged wet weather bring in the bulbs and dry them off in warmth indoors.

The aim is to dry the bulbs as quickly and thoroughly as possible. Handle them carefully to avoid bruises and cuts; damaged, diseased, or thick-necked bulbs should not be stored.

Onions and garlic can be plaited in ropes and hung up after drying. This is rather laborious, but it keeps individual bulbs separate, making it easier to select the size wanted for cooking, and there is less likelihood of disease spreading from one bulb to another. Alternatively the bulbs can be hung in woven, plastic or nylon nets or stockings, or stored in shallow layers in trays. They must not be put into polythene bags because the atmosphere becomes too humid, encouraging condensation and rotting. Inspect all bulbs regularly and remove any showing signs of disease.

Pumpkins, marrows, winter squashes

Pumpkins and other firm-fleshed gourds, which will keep for several months, are picked when mature but not over-ripe. Dry them off well in the sun to harden their skins before storing them in cool, dry, frost-free conditions. They can be placed on racks or suspended in nets. Cover them with extra sacking if unusually hard frost is expected.

STORAGE OF WINTER CABBAGES

1 *Stored in a cold frame, on raised wooden slats.*

2 *Hung in nets in a frost-free, well-ventilated shed.*

STORING ONIONS

1 *In a net bag; old nylon stockings will do as well.*

2 *Tied to a rope, the stringing half-completed.*

Drying vegetables

Beans and peas can be dried for winter use. A few plants are best reserved for the purpose, leaving the pods on the plants until nearly mature. The plants can then be uprooted whole and hung to dry in a cool, airy place, or, if more convenient, the individual pods picked off and left on trays to dry. Once dry they can be shelled and stored in air-tight jars. (They will need to be soaked in water for 24 hours before use.)

Hot pepper plants can similarly be pulled up and dried indoors. The peppers will remain in good condition for several years. Green peppers will keep in reasonable condition for several months if the plants are hung to dry in an airy frost-free shed.

DRYING BEANS

Hanging up french beans to dry: the whole plant is pulled up by the roots.

Planning and Siting

Most modern vegetable growers have little option about where to site their vegetable garden. The ideal site is an open but not exposed position, free from the damaging drips of overhanging trees, or from shade cast by tall buildings or trees, and is not a frost pocket. In exposed sites windbreaks should be planted or erected (see pp. 39–40).

If there is a choice the rows should run north and south, to make maximum use of sunlight. This is especially important with tall growing crops such as runner beans, so that they do not cast too much shade on neighbouring crops. However, on a steep slope it is always better to cultivate across the slope to minimize erosion.

Rotation

One element of planning is crop rotation, i.e. growing crops of one type on a different piece of land over a 3- or 4-year cycle. The main reason for rotation is to avoid the build-up of certain soil-borne pests (e.g. eelworms) and diseases (e.g. botrytis). Most pests and diseases attack only one crop, or a relatively narrow range of closely related crops; if these crops are grown continuously on one site, certain pests and diseases are likely to build up to a far more serious extent than if crops of different botanical groups were alternated on the site.

Certain crops, because of the way they are grown and their habit of growth help to control weeds. Potatoes for example leave the soil relatively clean because of their smothering leaf canopy and need for earthing up, which also disturbs the weeds.

For rotational purposes, the following are the important groups of vegetables. These are related botanically and crops within these groups tend to be susceptible to the same pests and diseases.

Brassicas. Brussels sprouts, sprouting broccoli, cabbages, calabrese, cauliflower, Chinese cabbage, Chinese and Japanese mustards, kale, kohl rabi, radishes, swedes, turnips.

Legumes. Broad beans, french and runner beans, peas.

Onions. Garlic, leeks, onions, shallots.

Carrots, celeriac, celery, parsley, parsnips.

Potatoes, tomatoes.

Other benefits from rotating crops relate to weed control and manuring; but these are secondary to the need to prevent a build-up of pests and diseases.

Gardeners often draw up very detailed garden plans, but in practice it is difficult to keep to them

DIAGRAM OF A SIMPLE THREE-YEAR ROTATION OF PRINCIPAL CROPS

	A	B	C
1st year	Peas Beans Onions, leeks Shallots, garlic Lettuces Spinach Spinach beet Celery, celeriac Tomatoes	Cabbages Cauliflowers Broccoli Brussels sprouts Kale Kohl rabi Chinese cabbage Swedes Radishes Turnips	Potatoes Carrots Beetroots Parsnips Salsify Scorzonera Chicory
2nd year	B	C	A
3rd year	C	A	B

N.B. There is inevitably some overlap between groups of crops related botanically and the rotation groups. Try to avoid growing potatoes on the part of the plot where tomatoes were grown in the previous year. Salad crops, sweet corn, marrows, beetroots, can be fitted in where convenient.

year after year, especially in small gardens. All plans should be considered flexible, but aim to keep within general principles of rotation:

1. Avoid following a crop with another from the same group for *at least* two years.
2. Watch for signs of build-up of serious soil pests or diseases. If any occur, don't grow susceptible crops on these sites because you will get a poor crop, and the problem will build up further. It may be necessary to avoid growing susceptible crops on such a plot for some years.

Within the overall requirements of the rotation it is always convenient to group together plants which are harvested at roughly the same time. This makes it easier to clear a reasonably sized piece of ground for sowing or planting.

Successional cropping and intercropping

To make the best use of a limited area, quick-growing crops can be fitted into empty spaces between the main crops, or between main crops before they have grown to maturity: see intersowing (p. 26) and intercropping (p. 33). Lettuces and radishes are among the most useful crops for successional cropping and intercropping as they can be fitted in in short rows in the garden to provide a continuous supply of young heads.

Continuity

Although for most people the main purpose of growing vegetables is to keep a constant supply for the household, in practice many gardens suffer from gluts and gaps. The gluts can be avoided by making a practice of successional sowing, sowing little and often, particularly of relatively fast-growing crops such as radishes, lettuces, turnips, spring onions, spinach. This gives a constant supply of vegetables to be used in their prime. It is also an insurance against pest and disease attacks and the unpredictability of the climate: while some sowings may fail, others will be successful.

Between February and May comes the so-called 'hungry gap' when few vegetables are maturing. Careful planning is required to ensure a supply of vegetables in that period.

The following normally mature at this season: sprouting broccoli, brussels sprouts, savoy and spring cabbages, winter cauliflowers, celeriac, chicories, endives, kale, leeks, overwintered lettuces, spinach, beet, swiss chard, turnips.

CONTINUITY

A well-planned and productive vegetable garden, showing leeks planted to follow the beans and tomatoes.

Pests and Diseases

A number of pests and diseases may attack vegetables and lead to failures of varying degree. Pests range from pigeons, sparrows, mice and moles to slugs, aphids, flies and weevils: diseases are caused by fungi, bacteria and viruses. Growing relatively large numbers of one plant can provide an easily available source of food for certain pests and diseases, and they may multiply rapidly.

The first line of defence against these problems is to grow plants well. Plants grown in clean conditions in fertile, well-drained soil, with adequate moisture and balanced nutrients, are less prone to pest and disease attack particularly of soil-borne diseases (e.g. damping off).

The incidence of pests and diseases varies from one locality to another. In most seasons it is only necessary to take preventive and control measures against the few most serious problems in the area.

General preventive measures

Soil condition. The importance of soil fertility and good drainage have already been discussed. Along with good feeding and watering they are of paramount importance in promoting healthy plant growth.

Garden hygiene. Clearing away plant debris, old cabbage stalks, rubbish and plant thinnings is important for practical as well as aesthetic reasons. Certain pests are attracted to, and take cover in plant debris and rubbish; pests and diseases overwinter on weeds and plant debris, and aphids overwinter in old brassica stalks, emerging in the spring to renew attacks. Always clear thinnings well away from a crop, as they attract the plant's natural pests. Those of carrots, for example, attract the carrot fly which lays its eggs in the thinned out rows. Diseased material and dead wood from the garden should be burnt.

Hand picking is a useful method of control for pests on a small scale: for example caterpillars can be picked off by hand in the early stages of an attack. Ladybirds can be collected and transferred to plants infested with aphids.

Cultural practices. Rapid germination and steady growth can offset damage by some pests and diseases. Sowing thinly in warm soil, in a well-prepared seedbed gets plants off to a good start. Some pests, such as the bean seed fly, lay eggs in freshly disturbed soil. By sowing in a 'stale' seedbed, i.e. allowing ten days to elapse between preparing the seedbed and sowing, severe damage can often be avoided.

Any thinning is best done as early as possible to avoid overcrowding. This and stagnant conditions can favour the spread of some pests and diseases. Methods of raising strong individual plants (such as using soil blocks) will avoid this problem.

Healthy plant material. Always ensure that plants bought in are healthy and free from diseases (such as clubroot on brassicas). Modern cultivars of some vegetables have been bred to have a useful degree of resistance or tolerance to common diseases. Seed is sometimes sold which has been treated with a fungicide against certain seed-borne diseases or against damping-off diseases. Take advantage of these developments.

Rotation (discussed later on pp. 47–8) is a useful means of limiting the incidence of certain soil-borne pests and diseases, in particular eelworm, and may be effective against some root rots.

Regular inspection. Inspect plants frequently so that pest and disease outbreaks can be spotted early when they are easier to control. Attacks can build up very rapidly if weather conditions are favourable to the pest or disease.

Handling. Handle vegetables for storage very gently as storage rots often start in bruises and cuts. This is particularly true of onions.

General types of pest and disease

Some of the more general pests and diseases and methods of control are discussed briefly here. Pests and diseases specific to particular crops are covered later under the vegetables concerned. For illustrations of some of the most common pests and diseases see pp. i–iii. Symptoms of damage and control measures are summarized on pp. iv–viii.

Pests

Birds. Large birds like pigeons and jays can seriously damage brassicas, peas and other vegetables, completely stripping the plants. Smaller birds such as sparrows destroy seedlings, pea plants and lettuces. Bird scarers are effective to some extent, but need to be moved frequently. Where persistent bird damage is encountered permanent wire or net cages may be the only solution. Small nets can be erected temporarily over vulnerable crops.

One or two strands of *strong* black cotton placed along a seed row an inch or two above the ground is very effective in preventing small birds from attacking seedlings when they emerge.

Insect pests. Wireworms, leatherjackets, cutworms, chafer grubs (the larval forms of click beetle, craneflies or daddy long legs, noctuid moths and chafer beetles respectively), along with millipedes, can be most serious soil pests, attacking the roots and stems of most types of plants and causing a high number of casualties.

They are generally worst in neglected gardens or after digging in grassland. Wireworm damage is most obvious the second year after digging in, as the pest feeds on decaying grass roots during the first season. These generally diminish with cultivation, but severe attacks can occasionally occur when conditions are favourable.

Chemicals such as diazinon, chlorpyrifos or bromophos can be worked into the soil before sowing or planting to control soil pests, but they may also kill some beneficial insects in the soil and so should only be used sparingly and only when necessary. Soil pests can be attracted to traps made from scooped out potatoes and carrots fixed on skewers just below the soil surface. Examine these daily, killing any pests found.

Aphids (greenfly and blackfly) are a large group of insects with many species and strains attacking vegetables. With a few exceptions each aphid species attacks only one species of plant. They feed on the sap of the plants, so weakening them and often transmitting virus diseases in the process. They can build up very rapidly in warm weather, although natural predators such as ladybirds and hoverfly larvae, natural parasites and fungal diseases help to keep down the populations.

Among the most common pests are several species of caterpillar which together with the maggots of the cabbage root fly are very damaging to brassicas. Carrots, parsnips and celery are frequently attacked by the maggots of carrot fly. In warm dry weather seedlings of brassicas and radishes are often attacked by the small flea beetles, which nibble round holes in the leaves and can be destructive if not caught early, though well-established plants can tolerate fairly extensive damage.

Eelworms, more correctly called nematodes, are minute unsegmented worms in the soil which cause a number of serious plant diseases and debility often referred to as 'soil sickness'. Some make cysts which enable them to hibernate in the soil for many years. As there are few remedies against eelworm the only practical solution is crop rotation, on a minimum three-year cycle.

Slugs and snails can be extremely damaging, being most active in wet weather and on heavy soil. They destroy and disfigure plants by eating holes in the leaves and stems of seedlings and mature plants. An effective means of catching them is to hunt for them by torchlight at night when they are feeding, pick them off by hand and destroy them. They can also be controlled chemically with methiocarb pellets (allowing a week before eating crops), metaldehyde pellets (which are less toxic) or the organic slug killer Fertosan.

Diseases

Diseases caused by fungi, bacteria and viruses are infectious and in favourable conditions may spread very rapidly through crops. Fungi cause various grey moulds, mildews, rots and galls, while bacterial infections tend to be slimy in nature. Virus diseases are often typified by stunted twisted growth and a mosaic pattern on the leaf. Fungi are spread by air-borne spores and sometimes resting spores which persist in the soil for years; bacteria may be spread in soil water, by splash dispersal and in wind-blown soil particles scattered by soil and wind; viruses are transmitted by aphids, other insects, eelworms, occasionally fungi and even by hand.

Once an attack is well established it is generally too late to eradicate the disease. Preventive spraying has to be done as soon as the first symptoms are apparent. Prevention is better than cure. Strict garden hygiene and burning all diseased materials, are important measures in containing and preventing further infection.

This is particularly true of virus diseases, for which there are no remedies. Infected plants should be uprooted and burnt.

Plants also suffer from 'physiological' disorders, caused by inadequate growing conditions. For example blossom end rot in tomatoes and also splitting of the fruits, is due to irregular watering; whiptail in cauliflower, where the growing point goes blind, is due to deficiency of the trace element molybdenum.

Chemical control

For several reasons chemicals should be used as little as possible in the vegetable garden:

- If wrongly used chemicals can be a hazard to man and wildlife. They must be handled carefully and the instructions for their use followed meticulously.
- Many chemicals leave residues on plants or in the soil, so a certain amount of time has to elapse before eating a treated crop.
- There is considerable risk of killing pollinating and beneficial insects as well as pests.
- Pests and diseases can sometimes develop immunity and resistance to specific chemicals, so the less they are used, the longer they are likely to remain effective. This is less likely to be a problem in a small garden than on a commercial scale, but it is as well to be aware of the possibility.

Chemicals are available as dusts (which are applied with puffers, or shaken up with seeds as seed dressings), granules (usually applied to the soil), and wettable powders and liquid concentrate to apply in liquid forms with small hand sprayers or syringes. A 2-pint sprayer (1 litre) is adequate for average garden purposes.

Insecticides operate either as *contact* or stomach poisons, killing only pests hit by the spray or which eat the plants within a few days after spraying, or as *systemics*, which are absorbed by the plant and kill those pests which feed on the sap.

Fungicides are less effective in controlling a disease once established, so have to be used in advance of an attack. *Protectants* kill infective spores which land on the plant surface, but are likely to be washed off by rain; *systemics* are absorbed by the plant and kill the fungus once it starts to grow inside the host.

Chemicals are marketed under brand names, but should be selected according to their *active ingredient*, stated on the bottle or packet of reputable products. The active ingredient is named in the recommendations for control given later.

Rules for spraying

Follow the manufacturer's instructions to the letter; never exceed the dose or frequency. Never spray in windy conditions (when spray can drift), or in hot sun (when the materials may scorch the leaves and pollinating insects are likely to be flying). Ideally spray in the evening or in dull weather. Try to avoid spraying plants in flower, as you are liable to kill pollinating insects. Never spray wilted plants, or water in ditches, tanks, tubs, etc. Spray so that the whole plant including the leaves is well covered, but never hold the sprayer nozzle so close to the plant or leaves that they are damaged.

Only make up the minimum amount of spray required and don't keep any left over for spraying later; wash out all equipment after use; never transfer spray material into ordinary bottles; keep chemicals well away from children and animals.

Biological control

There are a few cases where a pest or disease can be controlled by introducing one of its natural enemies. The best-known examples are the use of the predator *Phytosieulus persimilis* to control red spider mite, and the parasite *Encarsia formosa* for whitefly, both used in the greenhouse. The advantage of these methods of control is that they are 'natural' and specific, but they require some skill if they are to be operated effectively. Outdoors the bacterial spray Thuricide is used to control caterpillars.

Pests, Diseases and Disorders

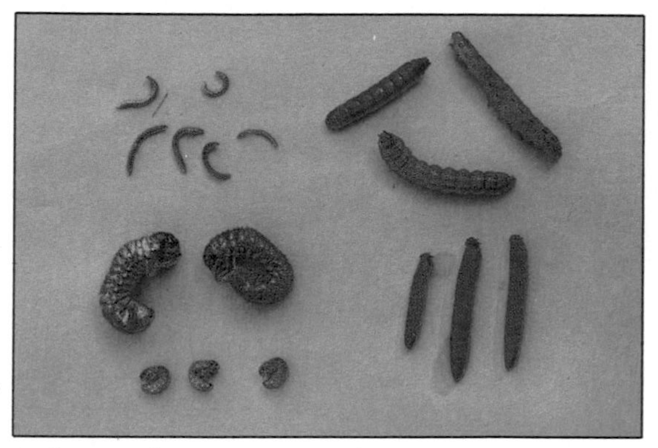

Soil pests: above wireworms (l), cutworms (r): below chafer grubs (l), leatherjackets (r): for symptoms and control see p. iv

Slug damage on lettuce and potato: for control see p. iv

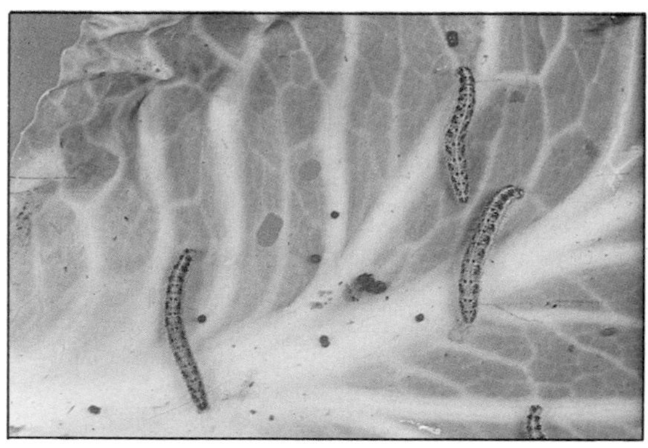

Large cabbage white butterfly caterpillars: for control see p. v

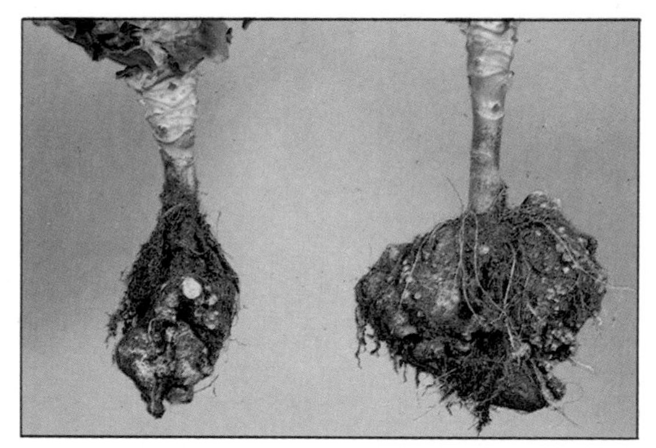

Club root of brassicas: for control see p. vii

Cabbage root fly maggots: for control see p. v

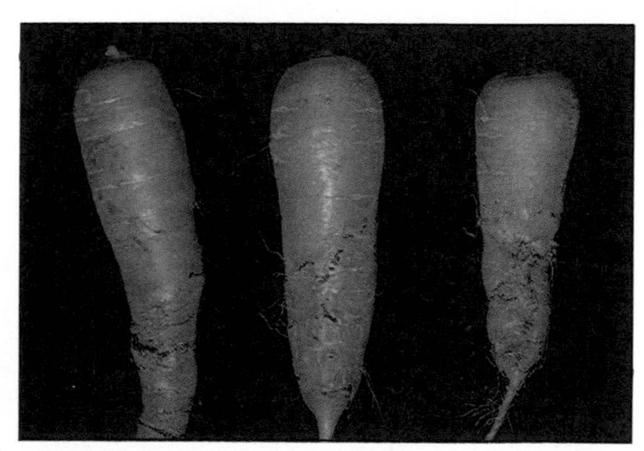

Carrot fly damage: for control see p. v

Celery leaf miner damage: for control see p. vi

Pod damage by pea thrips: for control see p. v

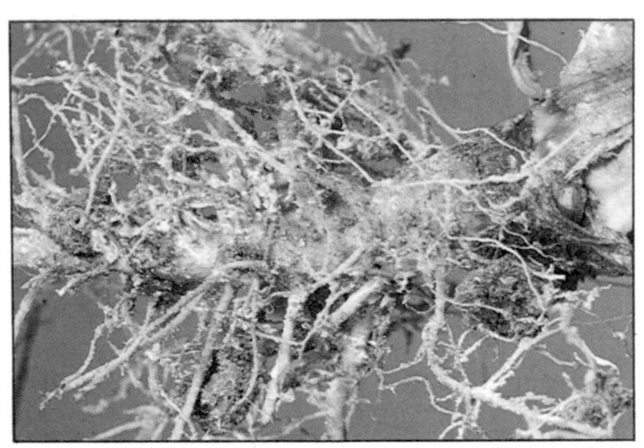

Lettuce root aphid: for control see p. iv

Lettuce downy mildew: for control see p. vii

Cucumber mosaic virus on a marrow: for control see p. viii

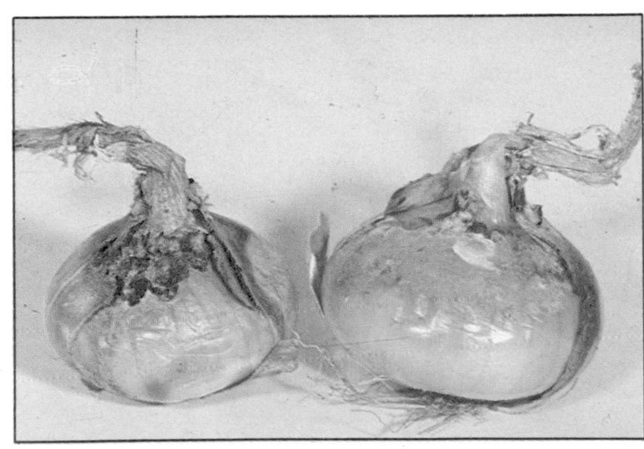

Onion neck rot: for control see p. vii

Onion white rot: for control see p. vii

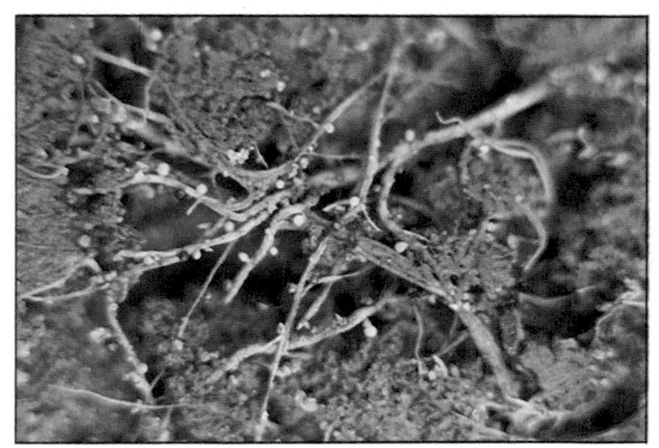

Golden potato cyst eelworm on potato roots (magnified): for control see p. vi

Potato common scab: for control see p. viii

Tomato blight: for control see p. viii

Blossom end rot of tomato: see pp. 47, 135

Magnesium deficiency on tomato: for control see p. 136

PESTS

Pest and appearance	Crop affected	Symptoms	Preventive measures	Chemical control
Wireworm: yellow wire-like body about 1 inch long (2.5 cm). See p. i.	Wide range of crops, especially roots, potatoes and lettuces.	Holes in roots and tubers; plants nipped off at soil level. March to September. Worst effects in first 3 years after cultivation of neglected ground.	Avoid growing root crops for 3 years after digging in turf.	Bromophos, chlorpyrifos or diazinon granules worked into top 2 inches of soil (5 cm) before sowing or planting.
Leatherjacket: soft legless, brown grub, up to 1¼ inches long (4 cm). See p. i.	Wide range of plants, young ones in particular, e.g. lettuces, brassicas.	Stems bitten through at soil level. Ragged feeding on lower leaves. March to July.	Ensure the ground is well drained. Clear and dig land before end of September, especially if after grassland.	As for wireworm.
Cutworm: greenish grey caterpillar up to 2 inches long (5 cm). See p. i.	Wide range, especially those with soft tap roots, e.g. lettuces, beetroots, carrots, parsnips, potatoes.	Cuts off plants at ground level. Makes holes in potatoes and other root crops. May to September.	Heavy rain or watering in June/July kills young caterpillars.	As for wireworm, but chlorpyrifos is the best to use.
Slugs and snails: soft-bodied creatures. See p. i.	Attack leaves, stems, roots, tubers, of a wide range of plants. Potatoes (maincrop) are at risk in particular.	Make holes in plant tissue. Most active on wet sites and in damp weather, all year round.	Improve drainage. Clear weeds. Lift maincrop potatoes as soon as the tubers have matured. Avoid highly susceptible cvs when slugs are a problem.	Slug pellets containing metaldehyde or, especially in damp conditions, methiocarb.
Black bean aphid.	Broad, french and runner beans.	Colonies of black aphids appear on stem tips. June to August.	Pinch out tops of broad beans after flowering. Transfer ladybirds on to colony.	Spray with derris/pyrethrum or systemic aphicide (e.g. dimethoate, heptenophos) or malathion or pirimicarb at dusk.
Lettuce root aphid. See p. ii.	Lettuces.	Waxy colonies of aphids on roots causing wilting and death. June to August.	Use resistant cvs, e.g. Avoncrisp, Avondefiance.	Apply diazinon dust or granules at planting. June to July.
Cabbage mealy aphid.	Brassicas including swedes.	Mealy grey aphid on leaves and stems. Leaves pucker. Worst attacks late summer, and can permanently stunt young plants.	Destroy overwintered brassicas by May. Move ladybirds to lightly infested plants.	Spray the underside of leaves with dimethoate, heptenophos, pirimicarb.
Leaf aphids.	Cucumbers, tomatoes.	Colonies of aphids on underside of leaves cause stunted growth and mottled puckered brittle leaves. June to September.	Brush off and destroy colonies while small. Destroy virus-infected plants promptly.	Spray with bioresmethrin, resmethrin, permethrin, pyrethrum or pirimicarb.
	Lettuces, endives.	Colonies on underside of leaves and in centre of plant: especially under cloches.	Aluminium foil mulch may deter winged aphids from landing.	Spray with dimethoate, heptenophos or pirimicarb; or derris near harvest.

Caterpillars. See p. i.	Brassicas.	Several species make holes in leaves. Frass collects at base of leaves.	Inspect plants twice weekly. Destroy eggs and caterpillars. Apply biological agent *Bacillus thuringiensis.*	Spray or dust with derris/pyrethrum, trichlorphon, fenitrothion, carbaryl or permethrin.
Asparagus beetle. Grey-green grubs, black and yellow adult beetles.	Asparagus.	Attack leaves and stems. Leaves may be stripped. Late May to October.	Remove beetles and larvae as soon as seen.	Spray with derris, malathion, or pirimiphos-methyl.
Flea beetle: bluish or black beetles $\frac{1}{8}$ inch long (3 mm).	Brassicas, radishes, swedes and turnips.	Neat round holes made in seedling leaves. March to September.	Sow early (March) or late (June) to miss most severe attack from first brood. Water seedling rows in dry spells to get seedlings quickly through this susceptible period.	Spray or dust seedlings with derris, gamma-HCH or pirimiphos-methyl.
Pea and bean weevil: greyish brown beetles about $\frac{1}{5}$ inch long (5 mm).	Peas and broad beans.	U-shaped notches nibbled from leaf margins. March to July.	Plants recover but seedlings may be checked.	If necessary treat as for flea beetle.
Pea thrips (thunderflies): black or yellow insects, just under $\frac{1}{6}$ inch long (2 mm).	Peas.	Attack young pods and foliage from early June. Worst in hot summers. Pods silvery, distorted. Flowers fail to develop. June to August. (See p. ii.)		Spray with fenitrothion or dimethoate.
Pea moth: small white caterpillars in the pods.	Peas.	Feed on developing peas. June to August.	Sow early (March) for crop to flower before early June.	For cvs flowering between early June and mid-August spray with permethrin, fenitrothion 7 to 10 days after first flowers appear.
Cabbage root fly: white maggots, $\frac{5}{8}$ inch long (8 mm).	Cabbages, turnips, swedes and radishes.	Maggot damage to roots causes stunting and death of seedlings and transplants. May to October.	Use a physical barrier round the plant stems after planting (see p. 70). Sow turnips and swedes after May to miss main attack.	Apply bromophos, chlorpyrifos, or diazinon granules to soil around plants within 3 days of planting or along seed drills.
Carrot fly: creamy white maggots $\frac{5}{8}$ inch long (8 mm).	Carrots, parsley, parsnips, celery, and celeriac. June to July.	Seedlings die. Plants become stunted and foliage reddish. The roots are mined and maggots will be found later, on lifting. (See p. i.)	Sow very thinly. Sow early (mid-March) or late (mid-June) to avoid first brood. Lift early carrots before September, parsnips and celery by November.	Apply bromophos, chlorpyrifos or diazinon granules 2 to 3 inches (5–8 cm) below seed row before sowing.

Pest and appearance	Crop affected	Symptoms	Preventive measures	Chemical control
Celery fly or leaf miner.	Celery, celeriac, lovage and parsnips.	Large blister mines in leaves (see p. ii). Early summer attacks more damaging; slows growth, makes stalks stringy and bitter.	Reject seedlings with blistered leaves. Pinch out and destroy blistered leaves.	Spray with dimethoate or trichlorphon if attack is becoming severe.
Onion fly: white maggots around base of bulb, $\frac{5}{8}$ inch long (8 mm).	Onions, leeks and shallots.	Seedlings die off in groups, with yellow drooping leaves. May to September. Worst on dry soils in hot weather.	Sow into 'stale' seedbed (see p. 46), especially for August sowings. Remove and burn infected plants.	If attacks occur frequently apply chlorpyrifos or diazinon granules along rows when seedlings at 'loop' stage.
Bean seed fly: white maggots, $\frac{5}{8}$ inch long (8 mm).	Runner beans, french beans.	Seeds do not germinate, or seedlings weak and distorted. April to October. Damage most frequent in cold wet soils, when germination is slow.	Sow into a 'stale' seedbed (see p. 46). Encourage rapid germination.	Apply dust or granules of bromophos, chlorpyrifos, diazinon, or gamma-HCH along rows at sowing.
Frit fly: small white maggot, $\frac{1}{8}$ inch long (3 mm).	Sweet corn.	Maggots attack base of seedling causing growing point to wilt and die. May to June.	Seedling immune after 5–6 leaf stage. Raise singly in pots in the greenhouse and transplant, or sow late (May).	Spray with fenitrothion or apply gamma-HCH dust as shoots emerge.
Stem and bulb eelworm: microscopic pests inside leaves and bulb or stem.	Onions, leeks and related plants.	Seedlings stunted, bloated and distorted. Later, leek stems thicken and rot; onions become thick-necked and rot. April to August.	Practise 3-year rotation. Remove and destroy infested plants. Keep weeds under control. All brassicas and lettuces are immune and can be grown in infested soil.	No chemical treatment available to amateurs.
Potato cyst eelworms: pinhead-sized spherical white or yellow-brown cysts on roots in July to August, see p. iii.	Potatoes, tomatoes.	Foliage stunted, weak and growth slow. Plants die early. Potato tubers and tomato fruits small.	Practise at least a 3-year rotation. Buy clean potato seed. Some cvs have some resistance to one of the cyst eelworm species.	No chemical treatment available to amateurs.

DISEASES

Disease	Crop affected	Symptoms	Preventive measures	Chemical control
Damping off.	Brassicas, beetroots, carrots, lettuces, peas, tomatoes.	Seedlings fail to emerge or keel over and die soon after emergence.	Avoid sowing in cold, wet soil. Sow thinly.	Dust seeds before sowing with a proprietary fungicidal seed dressing.
Root rot.	Peas, beans.	Leaves, stems and pods turn yellow and shrivelled. Roots and stem base become browny black.	Practise a 3-year rotation. Avoid sowing on a heavy wet soil (especially early cvs). Burn diseased plants.	Treat seeds with a proprietary fungicidal seed dressing. Disinfect soil with dazomet.

Downy mildew.	Brassicas.	Usually affects young plants. Leaves yellow with white area on under surface.	Avoid overcrowding. Raise seedlings in new beds.	Spray with mancozeb at first sign of disease.
	Lettuces.	Pale green or yellow angular areas on older leaves (white spores on lower surface). Infected areas die and become brown. Occurs mainly in autumn. See p. ii.	Use resistant cvs. Avoid overcrowding. Remove diseased leaves.	Spray with mancozeb or thiram.
	Onions.	Pale oval areas on leaves; tips of leaves become grey and die back. Leaves often fold downwards at infected area.	Avoid contaminated and badly drained soils. Ensure adequate air circulation.	Spray with thiram or mancozeb at first signs of disease.
Powdery mildew.	Cucumbers.	White powdery spots or patches on leaves.	Maintain good air circulation if under cover.	Spray with benomyl, dinocap, sulphur, triforine with bupirimate, or thiophanate-methyl at first sign of the disease.
Leek rust.	Leeks.	Orange spots and blotches appear on leaves. Occasionally very severe.	Raise plants on a fresh site each year. Remove and burn diseased leaves.	No chemical control known at present.
Clubroot.	Brassicas, swedes, turnips, radishes.	Above ground: discoloured leaves; wilting in warm weather. Below ground: solid swollen galls on roots. See p. i.	Maintain a slightly alkaline pH by liming. Ensure good drainage. Raise plants in sterile soil (e.g. soil blocks). Rotate brassicas strictly.	In bad cases sterilize the soil with dazomet but allow several weeks before planting. Dip transplant roots into calomel or benomyl or thiophanate-methyl.
Grey mould (*Botrytis*).	Lettuces.	Stems may rot completely at the collar, so that plant collapses. May be grey mould on leaves.	Destroy infected plants. Maintain good air circulation.	Spray with benomyl, captan, thiophanate-methyl, thiram at the first sign of the disease. Soil treatment with dicloran or quintozene before sowing or planting.
Neck rot.	Onions.	Grey rot on necks of stored onions. See p. ii.	Buy good-quality sets or treated seed. Dry bulbs well before storage. Remove rotting bulbs as seen.	Dust seed/sets with benomyl before sowing or planting.
White rot.	Onions.	White fluffy mould at base of onion and roots. Leaves wilt and turn yellow. See p. iii.	Rotation. Remove and burn affected plants.	Dust seeds with calomel or apply calomel to the row before sowing.

Disease	Crop affected	Symptoms	Preventive measures	Chemical control
Canker.	Parsnip.	Tops of roots blackened and cracked, and eventually rotted.	Rotation. Use resistant cvs, e.g. Avonresister. May/June sowings are often less affected.	No satisfactory chemical control known at present.
Leafspots.	Celery	Small brown spots on leaves and stalks. Yields may be poor in severe cases.	Use fungicide-treated seeds.	Spray with benomyl, copper fungicide, mancozeb, maneb or zineb.
	Beetroot, spinach beet, brassicas.	Brown spots on leaves, which may fall out leaving holes.	Rotate. Apply potash before sowing. Thin out early and/or space well.	
Blight.	Potatoes.	Brown patches on the leaves (showing in mid to late summer) which on the undersurface have a white fringe	Cut back haulms of infected potatoes in late August, to prevent blight spreading.	Spray maincrop cvs in early July with a copper fungicide, mancozeb, maneb or zineb.
	Tomatoes. See p. iii.	Brown patches on the leaves which soon die. Russet-brown marbled rotted areas on fruit.		Same chemicals applied to outdoor tomatoes as soon as the plant has been 'stopped'.
Common scab.	Potatoes.	Scabby areas on tubers, with ragged edges to lesions. See p. iii.	May be severe on light dry soils. Dig in organic matter but do not lime before planting. Grow resistant cultivars. Water in dry weather.	
Stem rot.	Tomatoes.	Yellow-brown canker at base of stem on mature plants. Black dots in cankered area.	Destroy infected plants.	Spray with benomyl or captan.
Cucumber mosaic virus. See p. ii.	Cucumbers, marrows.	Leaves mottled yellow with surface puckered and distorted. Plants become stunted and may die: fruits unlikely to develop.	Remove and destroy infected plants. Grow up to three times as many plants as finally needed.	Control of aphids will help to reduce virus spread.
Lettuce mosaic virus.	Lettuces.	Yellow mottling on leaves; veins appear transparent. Plants stunted.	Buy virus-tested seed. Destroy infected plants.	As above.
Leaf roll virus.	Potatoes.	Leaves roll upwards and become hard and brittle. Plants stunted.	Remove and burn infected plants. Use certified seed.	As above.
Mosaic viruses.	Potatoes.	Yellow mottling on leaves.	As above.	As above.
	Tomatoes.	Pale green and yellowish mottling on leaves. Fruit bronzed and blemished. Yields reduced.	Remove and burn infected plants.	As above.

Protected Cropping

The term protected cropping is used today to embrace the use of all forms of structure, permanent, semi-permanent and temporary, suitable for growing vegetables. They range from greenhouses, lean-to's and walk-in polythene tunnels to frames, cloches and low polythene tunnels. Here only growing in low-level protection without extra heating will be discussed. Some crops will need to be started with some extra heat. It should be stressed that only heated structures will give complete protection against frost.

Whatever the form of protection used, plant growth is improved partly because higher soil and air temperatures are obtained, partly because plants are protected against bad weather.

Protection is used:

- To extend the season of ordinary garden vegetables such as lettuces, carrots, peas, radishes, so that they can be obtained earlier or (sometimes) later than naturally.
- To get improved crops of half-hardy vegetables which do not perform well outdoors in an average British summer, e.g. tomatoes, cucumbers, green peppers.
- To improve the quality of hardy winter vegetables such as lettuce, endives and other hardy salads, spinach, chard, parsley, all of which are toughened by exposure to winter conditions.
- To give an early start to crops which will subsequently be planted outdoors.
- For miscellaneous uses such as hardening off seedlings, ripening tomatoes and onions, warming up the soil before spring sowings.

The various alternative forms of protection each has advantages and disadvantages. Portable frames, cloches and low polythene tunnels can be bought in small units: they are flexible in use, easily moved from one crop to another, and ventilation and watering are relatively simple. Among their disadvantages are that they require a fair amount of handling in erecting and moving, many crops cannot be grown to maturity in them because of their height, and only small areas of ground are protected by each unit.

Cloche materials

Each material too has advantages and disadvantages, glass and plastic being the two most commonly used. Glass transmits light well, but also retains heat very efficiently and at night retains more heat than plastic. As a result crops under glass are usually ready a few days earlier than those under plastic. Glass does not deteriorate with age, but glass cloches are heavy and cumbersome to erect and they are breakable. Glass is expensive initially.

A very wide range of plastic materials is used for cloches, for example PVC sheeting, acrylic sheet or Perspex, glass resin, fibreglass and semi-rigid materials. There are also wire-reinforced plastics.

Plastic materials can be transparent or translucent, rigid or corrugated. Some of the transparent materials transmit light exceptionally well, but it has also been shown that plants grow surprisingly well in the evenly diffused light beneath some translucent materials. Plastic does not retain heat as well as glass and temperatures under plastic are 2° or 3° lower than under glass. Plastic cloches are light in weight and usually need some method of anchorage.

One of the drawbacks of plastic is that it breaks down with age due to the action of ultra-violet light. Plastic should be stored out of sunlight when not in use. If possible buy a plastic material containing an ultra-violet inhibitor, so that it lasts longer.

Using cloches

The smallest and simplest cloches (of glass or rigid plastic) are tent-shaped. Larger, higher cloches with a tent roof supported on side pieces are known as barn cloches. Both can be placed in a line to cover the crop row, with the ends closed by a piece of glass held in place with a stick.

In general the larger the cloche the better for the crop. There must be enough room for plants to grow without being cramped; so barn cloches with their higher roofs are better than tent cloches for tall crops. Ideally foliage should not touch a glass surface – in summer it is liable to be scorched, in winter it may be frosted.

When plants have outgrown the cloche it can be placed on its ends on the ground and 'wrapped' around the plant, to give at least side shelter.

Ventilation. Temperatures build up very rapidly under cloches in sunny weather, and some means of ventilation, such as a panel which can be opened or rolled back, is useful. In some cloches glass or plastic panels can be removed and replaced with netting or are constructed with permanent netting beneath the panel. This allows for ventilation, with protection against birds.

CLOCHE TYPES

1 *Barn cloches with glass roof-panes partly open for ventilation: when the glass panes are removed, the netting prevents bird attacks.*

2 *Tent-type cloches suitable for low growing crops.*

3 *Corrugated plastic cloches, with a wire frame, make a simple low tunnel.*

4 *Rigid plastic sections with anchoring pegs make a continuous tunnel.*

CLOCHE TECHNIQUES

1 *Rigid plastic cloches with the end glass kept firmly in position.*

2 *Ventilation of a barn cloche: the glass pane is kept open by an angled wire.*

3 *Barn cloches 'wrapped' round an aubergine plant for protection.*

If no ventilation system has been arranged, cloches have to be moved slightly apart, or every other cloche removed, or cloches taken off the plants altogether during the sunniest part of the day.

Watering. Plants under cloches must be kept well watered. Larger cloches generally have to be moved for watering, though smaller cloches can often be watered from above, allowing the water to percolate through to the plants.

Low polythene tunnels

Low continuous tunnels, made from lightweight (150 gauge) polythene film sheeting stretched over galvanized steel wire hoops, pushed into the ground at about 3 feet apart (1 m), are the cheapest form of protective cropping for vegetables. The maximum height of the tunnels is usually between 13 and 18 inches (45 cm). Sheeting can be bought in rolls and cut to the length required. It is available in various widths, and it is advisable to err on the wide side to get maximum crop coverage and to allow for burying the sides if necessary.

The film is usually held taut over the hoops with strings, tied to eyes on either side of each hoop. If a permanent knot is made on one side and an easily untied knot such as a slip knot on the other, tunnels can be moved relatively quickly when the need arises. Thin wire hooked into eyes on the main hoops is sometimes used to keep the film in place.

The film is anchored at either end of the tunnel, either by burying it in the soil, or bunching it together and tying it in a knot around a short stake. The stake is put in the soil at a 45° angle about 2 feet (60 cm) beyond the last hoop.

Unless very securely erected, the sides of low tunnels are apt to be blown up in windy weather. This can be prevented either by weighting the sides with stones, clods or pieces of wood, or burying them in the ground. This does make the crops less easily accessible and less easy to ventilate.

Low tunnels are used and cropped in much the same way as cloches. They are easily moved, and are particularly useful in spring, autumn and winter. In mid-summer they tend to create a humid and close atmosphere which will encourage disease. They are relatively low in height, so are best used for low growing crops or for crops in their early stages.

For ventilation, watering and other operations the film is slid up between the hoop and retaining string – one side only for watering – both sides for maximum ventilation. In winter brush off heavy snow or the weight will crush plants; light snow, however, acts as insulation.

Polythene film lasts two or three years if handled carefully. Small tears can be repaired with plastic tape. As with other plastics, store it out of sunlight when not in use. The galvanized hoops last for years.

Strip cropping

The most effective way of using cloches and low tunnels is strip cropping. This is a system whereby, during the course of a year, the cloches or tunnels are moved to and fro between two or three strips of land preferably adjacent, so that they cover three or four different crops at their critical stages.

Numerous plans can be found in specialist books on gardening with cloches. One can easily draw up one's own on the assumption that one can sow or plant approximately ten days to two weeks earlier under cloches than in the open. A simple example of a two-strip system is given below.

Space under cloches is so valuable that inter-cropping, i.e. growing two or three crops together, should be practised wherever feasible, the faster growing crops being removed before the main crop requires the space. For example, radishes can be sown with most crops; while peas, dwarf french beans or sweet corn can be sown or planted down the middle of the cloches, with lettuce, radish, early carrots or early turnips sown down either side. The cloches are removed once the larger crops are well established.

Simple strip rotation with movable cloches

STRIP 1	STRIP 2
October to April	
Oct.: Hardy lettuce and radish sown at outside edges: intersown (*Nov.*) with early peas.	———
April to late May	
CLOCHES REMOVED	*April:* Dwarf beans sown under cloches.
May/June to October	
late May/early June: Bush tomatoes or green peppers planted under cloches.	CLOCHES REMOVED
October to April	
CLOCHES REMOVED	*Oct.:* Hardy lettuce and radish sown.

LOW PLASTIC TUNNELS

1 *Anchoring the end of the polythene tunnel by burying the end (left) and by tying it to a stake (right).*

2 *Ventilation by drawing up the polythene film between the wire and string.*

Frames

Frames can be permanent or portable, free-standing or lean-to. If orientated E–W, they are normally lower at the front and higher at the back, to catch the maximum light, varying from 7 inches to 1 foot (17–30 cm) at the front, and 9 inches to 1½ feet (23–45 cm) at the back.

Traditional frames were built with sides of brick, timber or concrete, many with 'Dutch light' roofs – a standard-sized sheet of horticultural glass in a wooden frame. Most modern frames are glass and aluminium, though some are constructed of plastic. See page 54.

Frames must be sited away from overhanging trees; for most purposes a south aspect is advisable.

Frames are relatively air-tight, and adequate ventilation is extremely important. Some frames have sliding panels, otherwise the glass covers (lights) must be propped open on warm days, and shaded or removed altogether in very sunny, hot weather. Lights must also have some means of being securely fastened, or they may blow off in windy weather. Frames can be covered with sacking or mats to keep out the frost in winter.

In winter water the soil rather than the crop, as water left on the leaves will encourage fungus infection.

In spring, frames are mainly used for early crops, for raising seeds and hardening off seedlings. In deep or shaded frames seed boxes may have to be raised off the ground to prevent them becoming drawn towards the light. In summer they are used for half-hardy crops such as tomatoes, cucumbers and melons, and in winter for hardy lettuces, over-wintered seedlings (e.g. cauliflower) and for blanching chicories and endives.

In winter and spring, watch out for mice; they soon discover crops in frames.

TYPES OF FRAMES

1 *Lettuces in a traditional Dutch light frame; the light is raised for ventilation.*

2 *An English light on a permanent brick-walled frame, particularly suitable for raising vegetables or forcing endive and chicory.*

3 *Lettuces in a movable aluminium and glass frame. The panes can be removed for ventilation.*

4 *A small frame with metal sides and rigid plastic top which can be removed for ventilation.*

Artichokes, Globe

Globe artichokes are handsome perennial vegetables. They are grown primarily for their thistle-like flower heads, in which the edible parts are the fleshy pads at the base of the bracts and the 'choke' or receptacle found in the larger heads. Plants are normally 2 to 3 feet high (60–90 cm), with a 3 foot (90 cm) spread.

Site/soil

Artichokes need an open but not exposed site, with protection from strong winds. The soil needs to be well drained, but the roots must not be allowed to dry out during the summer. Good crops are only obtained on fertile soil. Prepare the site by digging it thoroughly, incorporating plenty of well-rotted manure or compost.

Cultivation

Artichokes are normally raised from rooted suckers (offsets) taken in the spring from mature plants of good, named varieties, and planted out between February and April. They can either be purchased or taken from your own plants. Scrape away the soil from the base of the plant, and with a sharp-bladed trowel or knife slice down between the offset and parent plant. Select offsets with as much root as possible. Plant them firmly, about 2 inches deep (5 cm), and $2\frac{1}{2}$ to 3 feet apart (75–90 cm). The tips of the leaves can be trimmed back to reduce transpiration. Keep them well watered and protected from full sun until the plants are established. A dressing of general fertilizer can be given before planting, followed by a top-dressing of nitrogen six weeks later (see p. 11). Plants benefit from mulching throughout the growing season, and this will also help to smother weeds. Artichokes can also be raised from seed, sown indoors in February or outdoors in March. But seedling quality is very

PROPAGATION

Cutting offsets or suckers from the parent; in the foreground, good rooted offsets.

HARVESTING

Cutting the mature heads, a secondary head is seen below.

variable, and it is best to build up stock in the following years by taking offsets from the best plants, rejecting the poor ones.

During the first season of growth, keep the plants weed-free and well watered. A single head is produced towards the end of the first season.

Artichokes vary in their hardiness; they are more susceptible to cold when growing on a heavy soil. Some winter protection is normally advisable on any soil. In the north earth up the base of the plant, and cover the crown with straw or bracken. In the south leave the dead foliage to give some protection. Remove any covering in the following spring about mid-April.

In its second season the plant throws up several flowering stalks. Each shoot normally bears one large artichoke at the tip, and several smaller ones lower down the stem. If large heads are required, reduce these shoots to three per plant, snapping off the others at the base. These smaller artichokes can be removed when about 1½ inches diameter (4 cm) to encourage the growth of the terminal bud.

Plants generally start to deteriorate after their third season. It is good policy to replace about a third of one's plants each year with new offsets to maintain a steady supply of vigorous plants.

Harvesting

Artichokes can be eaten at various stages, but are normally considered mature when heads are plump, and the scales still soft, just before starting to open, and while the scales are still green. Cut off the heads with a portion of stem, or snap the stem off at the base if there are no secondary heads. Harvesting stimulates secondary shoots, which may give a second crop later in the season. This is encouraged if the plants are top-dressed with a nitrogen fertilizer (p. 11) and watered after the primary heads are cut.

Diseases

Petal blight fungus can cause rotting of the heads in wet weather. If it has been troublesome in previous years, start spraying with zineb or mancozeb soon after the buds start to develop and repeat at fortnightly intervals until 3 weeks before harvesting.

Recommended cultivars

The cultivar Vert de Laon is generally recommended as the most suitable for this country, and is usually available as offsets.

Artichokes, Jerusalem

Jerusalem artichokes are very hardy, perennial members of the sunflower family, grown for their nutritious, knobbly tubers. The plants grow to over 10 feet high (2.7 m).

Site/soil

Jerusalem artichokes tolerate open or shaded sites and a very wide range of soils, including cold, heavy soils. Because of the fibrous root system this is a useful crop for breaking in rough ground and heavy soil. They can be used to screen unsightly features, or planted in rows two to three deep, as windbreaks, but remember they are tall and will cast fairly heavy shade.

Cultivation

Plant tubers from February to May, 4 to 6 inches deep (10–15 cm), about 12 inches apart (30 cm). It is quite satisfactory to use tubers bought from a greengrocer. Those the size of a hen's egg are said to be best; larger tubers can be cut into two or three sections, provided each has a bud. When the plants are about 1 foot high (30 cm) the stems can be earthed up to make them more stable. In midsummer shorten back the tops to 5 to 6 feet (1.5–1.8 m), to encourage tuber growth and prevent them being windblown, which lowers the yields. Staking

JERUSALEM ARTICHOKES

An assortment of tubers after digging and cleaning.

or tying may be necessary to give extra support. In dry conditions jerusalem artichoke tubers will become more knobbly, so irrigate them if necessary.

When the foliage starts to yellow in autumn cut back stalks to within a few inches of the ground. The stalks can be left over the stumps, so helping to protect the soil from frost, and making it easier to lift the tubers in hard weather.

Tubers are normally lifted from the soil as required. Reserve a few tubers at the end of the season for planting; they can be lifted and replanted immediately. Dig up all other tubers however small, as jerusalem artichokes spread easily and become invasive.

Pests and diseases

The plants are not much troubled with these, although there is a fungal rot which may develop on stored tubers. If it should attack growing stems they become rotten for a foot or so above the soil surface. Burn such plants.

Cultivars

There are several forms of jerusalem artichoke, such as Fuseau and the red-skinned Boston, but they are not often offered by nurserymen. It may be possible to find them in local markets.

BEFORE WINTER

Cutting down the tops in autumn; tubers can be left in the ground for the winter.

Asparagus

Asparagus is a perennial vegetable, grown for its young shoots (spears). The plants can be productive for 8 to 20 years, and a dozen plants, well grown, would be sufficient for the average family.

Site/soil

Asparagus thrives on a wide range of soil types, from heavy clay to sand, provided it is well drained. It does not need particularly fertile soil. The preferred pH range is 6.3 to 7.5, so acid soils need to be limed. Very exposed sites and frost pockets should be avoided; asparagus should not be replanted where it has been grown before.

Cultivation

Asparagus was traditionally grown on ridged or raised beds, to give a long blanched stem. Today asparagus is grown very satisfactorily on flat beds, though ridged beds give better drainage and larger spears.

Where possible prepare the ground in the autumn before planting by digging thoroughly and incorporating a good dressing of well-rotted manure or compost. It is absolutely essential to rid the ground of every bit of any perennial weeds either by hand weeding or using weedkillers.

The quickest way of establishing an asparagus bed is to plant 1-year-old crowns, normally obtained from a nurseryman. These are far better than 2- or 3-year-old crowns, which, although larger, take longer to recover from transplanting. Handle the crowns very carefully and never allow them to dry out.

They should be planted in March or early April, at 4 inches deep (10 cm). Normally a trench 12 inches wide and 8 inches deep (30 × 20 cm) is taken out, and a mound about 4 inches (10 cm) made at the bottom of the trench. The crowns are laid carefully on this and covered with about 2 inches of fine soil (5 cm). The trench is filled in gradually during the season as the shoots grow. A top-dressing of fertilizer (high in nitrogen and potash, but low in phosphate) can be applied at planting. This can be given as an annual spring dressing. (See also p. 11.)

Asparagus can also be raised from seed, sown very thinly, in March in drills about 2 inches deep (5 cm). Plants are lifted the following spring and planted in their permanent positions, selecting the biggest crowns.

Asparagus is normally grown in single rows, with plants about 1½ feet apart (45 cm). Closer spacing

ASPARAGUS

The plants are placed on a central ridge in the trench.

Cutting down the asparagus fern in late October.

Cutting the shoots below ground level with an asparagus knife.

gives higher yields; wider spacing thicker spears. Beds can be made of two to three rows with paths of 3 feet (90 cm) between beds. Optimum spacing is $2\frac{1}{4}$ plants per square yard.

Individual asparagus plants are male or female. Male plants are higher yielding, but as it is impossible to distinguish them until the plants are more than a year old, most plantations are mixed.

During the growing season keep the beds weed free with hand weeding or shallow, surface hoeing, so as not to disturb the roots. Remove any asparagus seedlings. Where fern is liable to be blown over give it some support with canes and twine. After the fern has turned yellow in the autumn cut it down to within an inch of ground level (2.5 cm). If a 'long handled' spear is preferred, 2 or 3 inches of soil (5–8 cm) can be pulled up over the stumps. In heavy soils this can be done in spring.

Recent research has shown that there is no value in giving the beds a mulch of manure or straw in winter, nor in dressing them with salt.

Harvesting
Asparagus should not be cut until its third year, i.e. 2 years after planting 1-year-old crowns. Depending on the season and cultivar, cutting can normally start in the second half of April. When the spears are about 5 to 7 inches high (14–17 cm) cut the spears an inch or so below ground level, using a sharp knife. In the first season cut for no more than 6 weeks; in following years for not more than 8 weeks.

Pests and diseases
Slugs can be very damaging to young asparagus and should be controlled. The orange and black asparagus beetle and their larvae are destructive in some areas, defoliating the plants (see p. v). Beds sometimes become infected with violet root rot fungus, seen as purple strands on the roots. This also attacks weeds, carrots, potatoes and beet. As there is no remedy the ground should be left fallow or non-susceptible crops grown, for four years. The rest of the bed can be isolated by digging sheets of thick polythene 1 foot deep (30 cm) into the ground around the infected area. Violet root rot is a soil-borne disease which may become so severe as to require resiting of the bed.

Recommended cultivars
Giant Mammoth is recommended for heavy soil; Connovers Colossal for light or sandy soils.

Asparagus Pea

Asparagus pea is a pretty, decorative plant, with delicate foliage and scarlet-brown flowers. It belongs to the pea family, and is grown for the triangular-shaped, winged pods, which are cooked whole and are said to have a flavour of asparagus. The plants grow 12 to 18 inches high (30–45 cm), spreading to $1\frac{1}{2}$ to 2 feet across (45–60 cm).

Site/soil
Asparagus peas do best in an open sunny site on rich light soil.

Cultivation
Seeds can be sown outside from mid-April until the end of May, sowing so that plants are about 10 to 12 inches apart (25–30 cm) in rows at 15 inches apart (37 cm). Alternatively seed can be started indoors in April, transplanting outside in May. The growing plant only needs to be supported with small pea sticks or twigs, or twine attached to small canes.

Harvesting
Pods are ready for picking from June to August. Pick them when immature, between 1 and 2 inches long (5 cm), otherwise they become tough. Regular picking prolongs the season, as once the seeds in the pods start to harden, the crop is checked.

Yields are low in comparison with garden peas, but the flavour is excellent.

ASPARAGUS PEA

The fluted pods of asparagus pea, picked at a young stage.

Aubergine

Aubergine is a plant of tropical origin, and so will not tolerate frost. It has a bushy habit, growing about 2 to 2½ feet high (60–75 cm) and about 2 feet across (60 cm). The stems and leaves are prickly; the flowers a beautiful purple. The fruits, which are eaten immature, are round, long or oval, usually purple or black but white in some cultivars.

Site/soil

Aubergines are deep rooted, requiring fertile soil. If grown outdoors, which would only be successful in the south of the country, choose a sunny sheltered spot, ideally against a wall where they might be grown in a growing bag. Otherwise they need cloche or frame protection.

Cultivation

Seed can be sown in heat (about 70 °F – 21 °C) from the end of February to early April. Once the seedlings have germinated aim to maintain minimum night temperatures of 60 °F (16 °C) and day temperatures of 65 °F (18 °C) to keep the plants growing. Seedlings are ready for transplanting into pots when about 2 inches high (5 cm). Aim to grow short-jointed, sturdy plants with good root systems; overheating and forcing will lead to spindly plants.

Aubergines can be planted out in April or May under protection, or after risk of frost outdoors (end of May in the south). Plant them 16 to 18 inches apart (45 cm).

Growing plants need plenty of water. Nip out the tops when the plants are 15 inches high (40 cm) to encourage bushy growth. Plants may need staking and tying if growth is vigorous. Where there are several flowers on one stem, remove all but the largest after the fruit has set. A maximum of four fruits should be allowed on each plant. Once four fruits have set, surplus side shoots can be removed.

Plants will benefit from feeding with a tomato fertilizer every 10 to 12 days once the fruits start to swell.

Harvesting

Fruits are ready between July and September. Cut them off with a piece of stem when they have become plump and glossy.

Pests and diseases

When grown under cover, and to a lesser extent outdoors, red spider mite, whitefly and greenfly are troublesome. To help to reduce red spider mite populations give ample ventilation and sprinkle the plants regularly with water on hot days.

Recommended cultivars

Money Maker (F_1). There are numerous others on the market which are satisfactory.

AUBERGINE

An aubergine plant bearing flowers, and with a ripe fruit.

Beans, Broad

Broad beans are the hardiest of our beans, and are grown primarily for the large green or white beans within the pods. The very long-podded (Longpod) cultivars are the hardiest, but the broader, shorter Windsor group are considered better flavoured. The green-seeded cultivars freeze better.

The older cultivars reach heights of 3 to 5 feet (1–2 m); newer dwarf cultivars, with upstanding pods, are only about a foot tall (30 cm). They are very useful where space is limited or for growing under cloches.

Site/soil

An open site is best for the spring and summer sowings. A slightly sheltered position and well-drained soil is advisable for late autumn sowings.

Broad beans require a reasonably fertile soil, preferably well dug and manured in the previous winter, and they prefer a neutral to slightly acid soil. They should not be grown on the same site two years running, because of the risk of soil-borne foot and root rot diseases, which cause plants to collapse.

Cultivation

First sowings can be made as soon as the soil is workable in February or March. For successional crops further sowings can be made in April and May.

In mild parts of the country autumn sowings (late October and November) may give very early crops the following year. In some seasons the crop is lost due to soil pests and severe weather, in others they are only marginally earlier than spring-sown beans, but nevertheless it can be worthwhile. Aquadulce is particularly suitable for autumn sowing.

Overwintered and spring-sown crops benefit from cloche protection, particularly in the early stages. The dwarf cultivar The Sutton is suitable for autumn or spring sowing under cloches.

In cold areas, or where autumn sowings tend to fail, sow seed in boxes in greenhouses or frames in December or January, for planting out early in the year.

Sow seed outdoors at 1½ to 2 inches deep (5 cm), either in drills or using a dibber (taking care not to leave an air pocket beneath the seed). Discard any seeds with holes in them, generally caused by bean beetles.

Maximum yields are obtained at a spacing of 2 plants per square foot. Broad beans are often grown in staggered double rows, the seeds 9 inches apart (20 cm), with 2 foot paths (60 cm) between the pairs of rows. They can also be grown satisfactorily in patches 3 feet wide (90 cm), with equidistant spacing of 9 to 12 inches (20–30 cm) between plants. Tall varieties can also be grown at 4½ inches apart (11 cm) in rows 18 inches apart (45 cm).

Most beans require a support of canes and twine to prevent them being blown over when fruiting. The smaller cultivars can be propped up with twigs if necessary.

It is not necessary to water broad beans between germination and flowering, unless the plants are actually wilting. If rainfall is less than normal, watering once the beans start to flower and throughout the pod-forming and harvesting period, at the rate of 4 gal./sq. yd per week (22 litres/m^2) will give improved yields and better-quality pods.

When the plants are in full flower, or when small colonies of black aphids are noticed on the tops of the plants, the tips can be nipped out. This both encourages the development of the beans and discourages the blackfly.

Harvesting

Broad beans are often the first fresh vegetables of the season. Overwintered crops are generally ready for picking from May onwards, with later sowings cropping from June to August. Pick the pods before they are too large, or else the beans will have become tough. The very small pods can be used whole, but if many are picked small the total yields will be lowered. Broad beans can be dried for use during the winter.

Pests and diseases

Blackfly (see p. iv) is the major pest of broad beans. Bean weevils may also be troublesome (see p. v). The disease, chocolate spot, may also be troublesome, but vigorous well-grown plants are less susceptible to attack.

Recommended cultivars

For autumn sowing: Aquadulce, The Sutton (under cloches).

For spring and summer sowing: Express, Masterpiece, Green Longpod, Dreadnought (Longpods), Giant Four Seeded White Windsor, Witkiem Major, The Sutton (Windsors).

Red Epicure is a cultivar with well-flavoured red beans.

BROAD BEANS

Young plants of a dwarf broad bean grown in a bed showing equidistant row spacing.

Canes and string for support for taller varieties.

Pinching out the tops of the plants at flowering. If black fly is present they will also be removed.

Types of broad beans: left, Longpod, right, Windsor.

Beans, French or Kidney

French beans are half-hardy and treated as annuals. They are grown mainly for the pods, which are eaten when immature. However, when partially ripened they can be shelled and the fresh beans eaten. The mature dry beans, haricots, can be stored for winter use.

Most cultivars form bushy plants but there are also climbing cultivars. French bean pods display a wide range in colour, shape and length. The English forms are relatively flat and straight, with a tendency to stringiness as they mature; pods of the French cultivars are usually curved in cross-section, and generally stringless. Waxpod types and the purple cultivars are considered particularly well flavoured. French beans are self-pollinating, and do not have the problems of fruit-setting that may occur with runner beans.

Site/soil

French beans need an open but sheltered site, as they are very susceptible to wind damage. It is best to rotate them because of a possible build-up of root-rotting diseases. They prefer rich light soil, neutral to slightly acid. The soil should be well worked, ideally with manure or compost incorporated the previous season.

Cultivation

Most failures with french beans result from sowing too early in cold soils. Seeds will not germinate successfully until soil temperatures reach 50° to 54 °F (10–12 °C), which is normally late April to early May in the south of England, and about two weeks later in the north. If cold, wet conditions occur after sowing, beans frequently succumb to pests and diseases in the soil.

This problem can be overcome by sowing seeds in boxes, blocks or pots indoors, and transplanting them outdoors when 2 to 3 inches high (5–8 cm). Use healthy seed preferably dressed with a fungicide against soil-borne diseases. When sowing directly outside, prepare the seedbed 10 days before sowing and, if possible, warm the soil beforehand with cloches or a covering of plastic.

Sow the seed at about 1½ to 2 inches deep (5 cm), making successional sowings from the end of April until mid-July. Slightly earlier sowings can be made under cloches or indoors. The traditional spacing is to sow at 2½ to 4 inches apart (6–10 cm) and thinned to 9 inches (22 cm). But research has shown that the highest yields of french beans are produced at a density of 3 to 4 plants per square foot, with equidistant spacing between plants. To achieve this grow in rows 18 inches apart (45 cm) spaced at 2 to 3 inches (5–8 cm) in the rows, or in beds with 6 inches between the plants (15 cm). No thinning will be necessary later with these populations.

The plants will benefit by being mulched. For fertilizer requirements see pp. 10–11.

Climbing cultivars need supports (see runner beans), but bush cultivars can be supported with small twigs, to keep the lower leaves off the ground and the pods clean.

French beans benefit from extra watering once they are in flower. In dry conditions give 4 gal./sq. yd/week (22 litres/m^2). Pod set is improved, and stringiness delayed, if the soil is kept moist and the plants well watered.

Harvesting

The earliest cloche sowings are ready in June, while successional sowings can be picked from July until frost, or later if covered by cloches. Pick the pods in their prime, when they can be cleanly snapped in half. Frequent picking will encourage higher yields and better quality.

If dried beans (haricots) are required, select a few plants and leave the pods unpicked until they have turned brown. The whole plant can then be pulled up and hung in a dry airy shed (see p. 43). When the pods have dried to the point of cracking open, shell them and store the beans in air-tight jars.

Pests and diseases

The main pests are slugs, bean seed fly (see p. vi) and black bean aphid (see p. iv). Various diseases include foot and root rots, anthracnose, halo blight and virus. Rotation, the use of healthy seed and good growing conditions are the main precautions against these. Diseased plants should be removed and destroyed.

Recommended cultivars

Bush varieties: Cascade, Loch Ness (for colder areas), Masterpiece, Prince, Pros Gitana, Sprite, Tendergreen.
Climbing: Early Blue Lake.
For drying: Chevrier Vert.
Waxpods: Kinghorn Wax.
Purple: Royal Burgundy.

FRENCH BEANS

Earthing up the young seedlings at an early stage of growth.

French beans at the stage when they should be thinned.

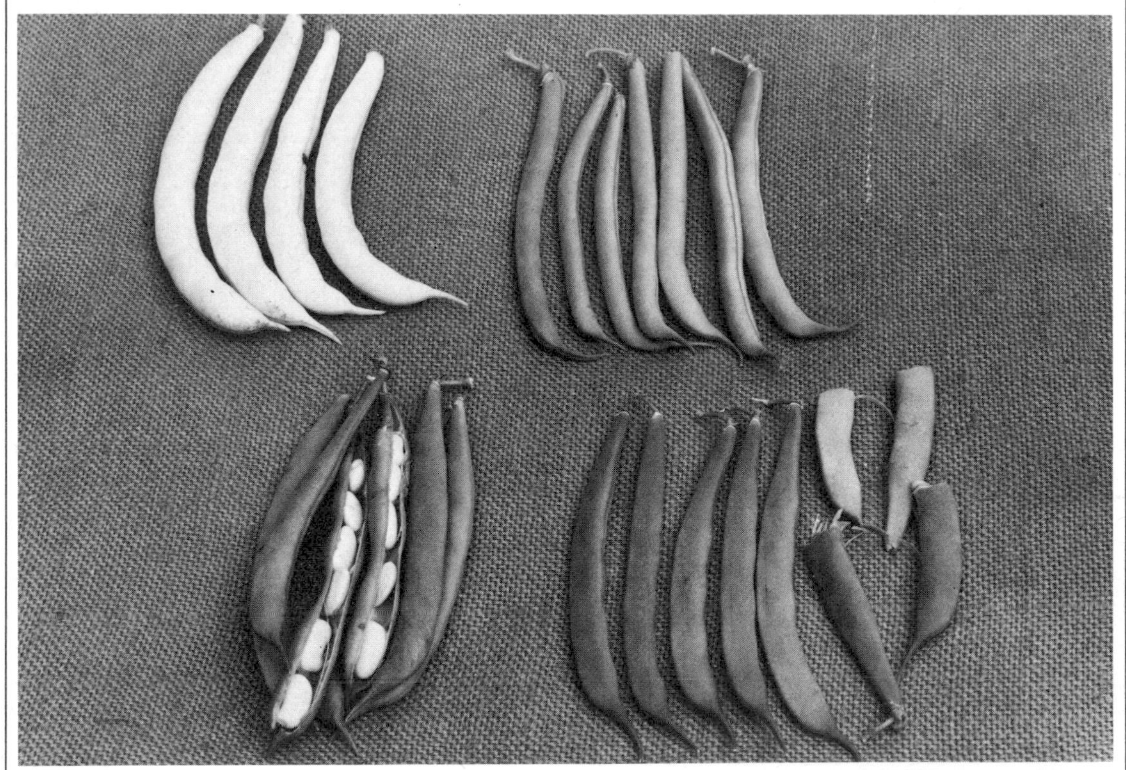

Types: top left, waxpods, right, flageolet, below left, rounded stringless types and, right, flat (showing stringiness, when broken).

Beans, Runner

Originally introduced into this country for its ornamental qualities, the runner bean is one of our most prolific and vigorous vegetables. It bears heavy crops of long, flat-podded beans from July to October. Most varieties are climbers, reaching heights of 8 to 10 feet (3 m), making it a useful screening plant. There are some dwarf forms.

Site/soil

Runner beans are susceptible to frost, and so are not generally successful in colder parts of the country. They benefit from planting in warm sheltered positions, for example growing up a fence. A warm site also encourages pollinating insects, which help the beans to set. It is better not to grow runner beans in the same position year after year, because of the likely build-up of root-rotting diseases.

They are deep-rooting plants, requiring well-prepared, fertile, moisture-retentive soil. The ground is best prepared in the previous autumn, ideally digging a trench one spit deep and 24 inches wide (60 cm), into which strawy manure or compost is mixed when replacing the top soil.

Cultivation

Runner beans need relatively warm soil for germination, at least 50 to 54 °F (10–12 °C). It is better to wait until the second half of May before sowing, or into June in the north. They can also be started indoors in early May and transplanted at the end of the month.

Highest yields are obtained from planting at a density of 2 plants per square foot. Runner beans are usually grown in double rows, at 2 feet apart (60 cm), with plants 6 inches apart (15 cm) in the rows.

Very sturdy supports need to be erected for climbing runner beans. Traditionally crossed poles or bamboo canes at least 8 feet long (2.5 m) are used, firmly secured to cross members along the top. There should either be one cane per plant, or provided there are canes or poles every 2 feet (60 cm), strings can be substituted for intermediate plants. Run the strings from the ridge to a horizontal string linking the canes a few inches above ground level. Alternative means of support are 4 inch square wire or nylon netting (beans will not grip plastic-coated netting), or circular wigwams of canes, poles or strings, tied near the apex. Tension wires may be necessary at either end of a supporting structure to bear the weight of the crop.

Climbing forms can be grown without support

RUNNER BEANS

Preparing the trench for planting the beans, manure being dug in.

Nipping off the tops of climbing beans to make them dwarf.

by nipping out the tips once they start to throw climbing shoots. This lowers the yield, but the plants bear sooner and set more readily.

Problems are sometimes encountered in getting flowers to set. Contrary to popular belief, syringing flowers with water does not help setting; however, watering the soil at the base of the plant has a beneficial effect on flowering and pod setting. In dry weather the plants will need 1 to 2 gal./sq. yd (5–11 litres/m^2) twice a week during these periods.

Harvesting

Runner beans crop from about July until October and beans *must* be picked regularly and thoroughly to obtain the highest yields, and to prevent pods from becoming tough and stringy. Mature beans can be dried for use in winter.

Pests and diseases

The main pests are slugs, bean seed fly (see p. vi) and black bean aphid (see p. iv). Various diseases include foot and root rots, anthracnose, halo blight and virus. Rotation, the use of healthy seed and good growing conditions are the main precautions.

Recommended cultivars

Achievement, Desiree, Enorma, Fry, Kelvedon Marvel, Mergoles, Prizewinner, Red Knight.

SUPPORTS FOR CLIMBING BEANS

A wigwam of bamboo canes at least 8 feet long, tied securely at the top.

The traditional support of poles firmly secured to a cross member.

Beans supported by nylon netting with rigid side and top supports.

Beetroot

Beetroot is one of the most useful root vegetables, used fresh in summer, or stored or pickled for winter. There are cultivars that are round, long, or an intermediate oval in shape. Round forms are used for both summer and winter supplies, while the slower growing, but perhaps better flavoured, long types are normally stored for winter use. Beet is usually deep red-purple in colour, but the less common yellow and white forms are well flavoured.

Site/soil

An open, unshaded site is best. Beets need rich, light soil, manured the previous season, *not* freshly manured. Long-rooted varieties require deep soil. The preferred pH is slightly acid to alkaline, so the soil should be limed if acid.

Beetroot are susceptible to mineral deficiencies, particularly boron, manganese and magnesium (see p. 12).

Cultivation

The beet 'seed' is made up of several seeds, containing a natural inhibitor which sometimes limits germination. It can be soaked out by immersing the seed for half an hour in tepid water before sowing. Alternatively use thiram-treated seed if available, as the treatment soaks out the inhibitor and frees the seed of certain fungal diseases. Beetroot seed will not germinate at a soil temperature below 45 °F (7 °C), and in cold soils sowings in early spring are often slow to emerge.

Some cultivars of beet are liable to bolt (run to seed), if sown too early in the year or when conditions have been difficult for germination. For early sowings use a bolt-resistant cultivar and, if possible, warm the soil with cloches before sowing. Seedlings can also be raised indoors, preferably in blocks, to be planted out when about 2 inches high (5 cm), or sown by the fluid-sowing technique.

Beetroot can be sown in rows or in patches with equidistant spacing between plants. Sow seed in drills ½ to ¾ inch deep (12–18 mm). Sow as thinly as possible, although some thinning may be necessary later. Sparrows attack beet seedlings, so net the rows or protect them with black cotton after sowing.

For early beet, which needs wide spacing to grow quickly:

Either

sow in late February/early March under cloches or in frames, using a bolt-resistant, round cultivar; aim for 5 plants per sq. foot, i.e. 3½ inches apart (9 cm) in rows 8 inches apart (22 cm). These are lifted at the end of May/early June.

Or

sow in late March/early April outdoors, using a bolt-resistant, round cultivar at the same spacing as above. This gives medium-sized beet in June and July.

For summer supplies and winter storage, use any cultivars, sow outdoors in May and June, in rows 12 inches apart (30 cm), with an inch (2.5 cm) between the beetroot.

For pickling beet aim at a maximum density of 20 plants per sq. ft.

For late autumn supplies and winter storage, sow outdoors in late June/early July, using a round cultivar, in rows 8 inches apart (22 cm), and 3 to 4 inches apart within the rows (8–10 cm).

In good conditions, round beet can be ready 11 to 13 weeks after sowing making a useful catch crop.

For steady growth and good-quality beet, water so as to prevent the soil drying out, at the rate of 2 gal. per sq. yd (11 litres/m^2), probably every 2 to 3 weeks in a dry season. Overwatering encourages leaf rather than root growth. For fertilizer requirements see pp. 10–11. Apply only part of the nitrogen requirement before sowing.

Harvesting

Beets are pulled when they reach the size required. On well-drained soil in mild areas beetroot can be stored in the soil during the winter, after cutting off the tops and covering the area with a layer of bracken or straw. If dug for storage lift the roots carefully in October with a fork, and twist off the stems an inch or so above the root. Store in boxes of moist sand indoors (see pp. 40–1).

Diseases and disorders

Damping off (see p. vi) and leafspots (p. viii) are the main disease problems with beetroot. The plants may also suffer from certain mineral deficiencies if organic material is not regularly supplied to the soil.

Recommended cultivars

Bolt-resistant round cultivars for early sowing: Avonearly, Boltardy, Detroit-Regala.
Bolt-susceptible round cultivar for late sowing: Detroit-Little Ball.
Long cultivars: Cheltenham Green Top, Cylindra.

BEETROOT

Thin sowing of maincrop beetroot.

Early beetroot sown on the bed system, aiming for 5 plants per square foot.

Beetroot harvested at the right size for pickling, about $1\frac{1}{2}$ inches in diameter.

Maincrop beetroot lifted for storage: the tops are twisted off to avoid 'bleeding'.

Brassicas: leaf crops

The brassicas are the backbone of the English vegetable garden, and include cabbage, sprouting broccoli, brussels sprouts, cauliflower and kale – and also the root crops swedes, turnips and kohl rabi (see pp. 128–9 and 96, respectively). The leafy crops in the first group have many features of cultivation in common which are summarized here.

Site/soil

Brassicas need an open unshaded site. The soil must be fertile, well drained and moisture retentive. Most brassicas prefer a slightly acid soil, but a very acid soil will need liming. The nitrogen requirements of these leafy crops are relatively high, mainly because they are growing over several months. The ground should be well worked and manured, ideally in the autumn before planting, but at least for the previous crop. It is not necessary to fork over the ground before planting: it is enough to clear the ground of weeds and plant debris without disturbing the soil. This gives the firm roothold brassicas need. Most brassicas take a relatively long time to mature, and are likely to need a top-dressing of a nitrogenous fertilizer during growth (see pp. 10–11).

Brassicas are prone to some soil-borne infections such as clubroot and brassica cyst eelworm so should be rotated over a 3 year cycle at least.

Cultivation

Most brassicas are sown in seedbeds and transplanted into their permanent positions in spring and early summer as ground becomes vacant. They can also be raised successfully in boxes, pots or soil blocks for planting out.

Sow seed at ¾ to 1 inch deep (2–2.5 cm), as thinly as possible, aiming to space the plants at 3 inches apart (7 cm). This will give them enough room to grow well and make strong transplants. Before lifting the plants for transplanting, water the seedbed to minimize root damage.

Good anchorage and stability are important factors in growing brassicas successfully. On light soils it is advisable to make drills about 3 inches wide (7.5 cm), and 4 inches deep (10 cm), planting in the bottom of the drill. Soil can be pulled up around the plant as it grows until the drill is level. On heavy soil brassicas are planted on the flat (as the drill might become waterlogged), with the lower leaves just above the soil level. In both cases plant firmly, so that if a leaf is tugged, it will tear off, rather than the plant being uprooted. Again, as the plant grows, soil can be hoed up around the base to give better support.

Where cabbage root fly is usually a pest, put discs of flexible material, e.g. carpet underlay, about 6 inches in diameter (15 cm) around the plant stem on the soil surface immediately after planting (see p. 70). An alternative 'physical' preventive is a bottomless plastic cup slipped over the newly planted brassicas and pressed down into the soil. The adults normally lay the eggs on the soil surface near to the host plant, so the barrier acts as a deterrent and also in addition it provides a home for the beetles which eat the fly eggs.

Water round the base of the plant immediately after transplanting. If conditions are dry in the 3 or 4 weeks after planting, water each plant, giving about ¼ pint (140 ml) a day, until they are well established.

In exposed positions, some of the taller growing overwintered brassicas (especially brussels sprouts and sprouting broccoli) may need to be securely staked in autumn to prevent 'windrock' at the base.

Keep plants weed free by hoeing during the growing season. Mulching helps to conserve moisture and suppress weeds. Catch crops of radishes or lettuces can often be grown between widely spaced brassicas, if sown or planted soon after the brassicas are planted.

Watering

If maximum yields and tender succulent crops are to be obtained, brassicas should never be checked by lack of water or nutrients. So frequent watering is beneficial, up to 4 gal./sq. yd/week (22 litres/m^2) in dry weather. Where facilities for watering are limited, the most effective means of watering is a single heavy watering 10 to 20 days before the crop matures.

Pests and diseases

Unfortunately brassicas are prone to a fair number of pests. The most common are *flea beetle*(p. v), which attacks the seedlings, *cabbage root fly* (pp. i, v), which usually attacks shortly after planting out, and *caterpillars* (pp. i, v) and *white mealy aphids* (p. iv) which damage the mature crop. Slugs and snails are sometimes very damaging, as are birds, especially pigeons, which may in some areas make it necessary to net the crop. The most serious disease is clubroot (pp. i, vii). In all cases, see pp. i–viii, for symptoms and preventive and control measures.

BRASSICAS

Lifting seedling brussels sprouts from the seedbed (after watering) for transplanting.

Planting out in a drill with a trowel.

A disc of carpet underlay placed around the stem to prevent attack by root fly.

Earthing up the stems to give firmer anchorage.

Broccoli, Sprouting

The purple and white sprouting broccolis are among the hardiest and highest-yielding brassicas, producing abundant, long, edible flower heads in spring. In fertile soils they can grow to dimensions of at least 3 feet high (90 cm) and 3 feet across (90 cm). The purple forms are hardier and more prolific than the white; there are early and late cultivars in both. Broccolis have an excellent flavour fresh, and freeze well. (For the green, summer-flowering broccoli, which is not hardy, see *Calabrese*; p. 78.)

Site/soil

See *Brassicas, General*. Sprouting broccoli does best in a warm, well-drained position.

Cultivation

Sow from mid-April to mid-May, sowing the earliest forms first to give a prolonged season. Plant out at 2 feet apart each way (60 cm) in June and July, aiming to complete planting by mid-July.

Sprouting broccoli develops into a large, top-heavy plant, so stalks should be earthed up during the growing season, and the plants may need to be firmly staked in the autumn. They are very likely to need protection from pigeons in winter.

For planting methods, watering, pests and diseases see *Brassicas, General* (pp. 69–70).

Harvesting

The season for sprouting broccoli normally extends from February to May, depending on area and cultivar. Snap off the flowering shoots about two-thirds down their length, when they are between 4 and 12 inches long (up to 30 cm), and before the flower buds open. New side shoots will be produced, and with regular picking, plants may continue cropping over 6 to 8 weeks.

Recommended cultivars

Early Purple, Late Purple; Early White, Late White.

SPROUTING BROCCOLI

A good plant of purple sprouting broccoli. Both this and the white broccoli are valuable winter crops.

White sprouting broccoli is harvested at the same time as the purple.

Brussels Sprouts

Brussels sprouts, the traditional British winter vegetable, can provide fresh pickings from September to April. They survive all but the most severe winters. The modern F_1 hybrids are a great improvement on earlier cultivars, as the sprouts are compact and uniform, few become loose or 'blown', the plants are more responsive to fertile conditions and are less likely to fall over in winter. Small button cultivars are excellent for freezing.

Site/soil

It is most important to plant in firm ground, which has *not* been freshly manured, as too much nitrogen will cause the sprouts to become loose. But brussels sprouts need an adequate supply of nitrogen throughout the relatively long period of cultivation: a base fertilizer dressing can be hoed in before planting, and a nitrogenous top-dressing supplied in late summer (for rates see p. 11).

Cultivation

Brussels sprouts grow over a period of several months and need to be kept growing steadily. Sow from mid-March to mid-April, progressing from early to late cultivars. For a very early crop (ready in August), seeds can be sown under glass in February or in early August of the previous year, planting out in spring.

Plant out from mid-May to early June. The usual spacing is between 2 and 3 feet apart (60–90 cm); the wider spacing produces large sprouts, which can be picked in succession over a long period. Closer spacing tends to induce smaller sprouts, and uniform maturity. Early, autumn maturing, F_1 cultivars for freezing can be planted at 20 inches apart (50 cm). After planting, water until the plants are established. (See *Brassicas, General.*) Subsequently, because of the wide spacing, little extra watering is required except in unusually dry years.

BRUSSELS SPROUTS

A young brussels sprout staked and earthed up.

Harvesting the sprouts, starting picking from the bottom of the stem.

Plants must be earthed up. They can be intercropped in the early stages.

The traditional practice of 'stopping' sprouts, i.e. taking out the growing point in late summer, is not now recommended for normal open pollinated or late maturing F_1 cultivars. However, autumn maturing F_1 cultivars grown for freezing can be stopped when the lowest sprouts are reaching $\frac{3}{4}$ inch diameter (2 cm), to encourage even development of the sprouts. This gives a uniform crop for picking at one time. If left unstopped a succession of sprouts can be picked over a longer period.

Harvesting

The earliest crops are ready in September. Pick from the bottom of the plant upwards, snapping off mature sprouts with a downward movement. When picking, remove blown sprouts, and yellow and diseased leaves. At the end of the season the sprout tops can be picked. They can become very weighty and are well flavoured.

Pests and diseases

See *Brassicas, General.* Clubroot (pp. i, vii), damping off (p. vi) and downy mildew (p. vii) are the most likely diseases. Of the normal range of brassica pests, attacks of mealy aphid (p. iv) in late summer can be particularly damaging, penetrating and spoiling the sprouts.

Recommended cultivars

Early (September–October): Lancelot F_1, Peer Gynt F_1, Topscore F_1.
Maincrop (October–December): Citadel F_1, Cor (Valiant) F_1, Mallard, Perfect Line F_1, Predora F_1, Roodnerf- Seven Hills, Widgeon.
Late (January–March): Achilles F_1, Fortress F_1, Rampart F_1 (very hardy), Sigmund F_1.

A plant of a modern cultivar with good, firm, evenly spaced sprouts.

A poor plant, with blown, overcrowded sprouts.

Cabbage

Fresh cabbage can be grown in the garden all year round, using the different types available. In addition there are the Dutch winter white varieties which can be cut and stored for winter, red cabbage, which besides being an undervalued cooked vegetable is used for pickling, and the recently introduced Abyssinian cabbage 'Karate', best used for 'greens' in spring and autumn.

All these cabbages are cultivated in the same way (for soil, site, cultivation, watering, pests and diseases see *Brassicas, General*), but sowing and planting dates, and suitable cultivars for each season, vary. These will be outlined below, grouped according to the main season of use. In practice there is considerable overlapping between the groups and in the use of any one cultivar. There are many excellent ones from which to choose.

SPRING CABBAGE

These are mostly small cabbages, with either round or pointed heads, for use in April/May. Most cultivars can also be eaten before they heart up, as leafy 'spring greens'. A base dressing is unnecessary when planting out spring cabbage, but a nitrogenous top-dressing in March or April, and watered in, is recommended (see p. 11). Spring cabbages should be well earthed up during the winter. Sow in a seedbed towards the end of July (in the north) or the first two weeks of August (in the south). Plant out from mid-September to mid-October, in rows 12 inches apart (30 cm) and 4 inches apart in the rows (10 cm). Use the two intermediate cabbages as spring greens, leaving the plants 12 inches apart (30 cm) to heart up. For a succession spring cabbage can also be sown in a cold frame or under cloches in September, planting them out in spring.

Recommended cultivars (those marked ★ are suitable for use as heads and as spring greens).
April, Durham Early★, Durham Elf, First Early Market 218★, Offenham Compacta.

SUMMER CABBAGE

The typical summer cabbage is a round compact cabbage with few outer leaves, for use from the end of June until September/October. They can be sown and planted in succession to give mature heads over a long season. Varieties which stand well without deteriorating are especially useful. Spacing can be varied according to the size of head required: planting at 14 inches apart each way (35 cm) gives small heads; 18 inches apart each way (45 cm) large heads. General fertilizer can be worked in before planting, but the plants are likely to need a top-dressing later in the growing season (see p. 11).

The main sowings are made outdoors in seedbeds from March to early May, starting with early summer cultivars, and progressing to late summer cultivars, for planting out in May and June.

Very early crops of early summer cabbage are obtained by sowing under glass in heat at the end of February (in the south) or the second week in March (in the north), to be planted out after hardening off.

Early summer cabbage can also be sown in heat, cold frames or under cloches, to avoid bolting, in February or March for planting out in late April or early May.

Recommended cultivars

Early summer round: Derby Day, Golden Acre-Progress, Marner Allfruh.
Early summer pointed: Hispi F_1, Cape Horn F_1.
Late summer round: Green Diadem F_1, Market Topper F_1, Marner Allfruh, Minicole F_1 (very long standing), Stonehead F_1 (long standing).
Late summer pointed: Hispi F_1.

WINTER CABBAGE

There are several fairly distinct types of cabbage for use during winter (November to March). The smooth-leaved drumheads are generally used up to Christmas, followed by semi-savoy January King types, with slightly curled leaves, cropping from December to February. Last to come in are the extremely hardy, crinkly leaved savoys, which stand through winter until March. The solid headed Dutch winter white types are cut in November for storage.

Sow outside from end April to mid-May, for planting out in July and early August. Standard spacing is about 18 inches apart each way (45 cm) smaller heads are obtained with closer spacing, and larger heads with wider spacing. Winter cabbages should be earthed up well and old leaves removed.

Cabbages for storage are lifted in late autumn and loose outer leaves removed. Inspect the heads periodically during the winter, removing any rotting outer leaves by rolling them back gently. Stored cabbages should always be handled extremely carefully to prevent bruising which may result in rotting. The cabbages need to be stored in a frost-free and dry place: methods of storage are described and illustrated on pp. 41–2.

CABBAGES

Spring cabbages in early April. These have headed and are ready for cutting.

A bed of spring greens in mid-February, ready for cutting.

Cutting a cross in the cabbage stalk, after harvesting the first head.

About five weeks later four small heads have been produced. This can best be done with spring and early summer cultivars.

Recommended cultivars

For use fresh: Aquarius F_1, Christmas Drumhead, January King. Savoy: Ice Queen F_1, Wirosa F_1. White cabbage × Savoy: Celtic F_1, Celsa F_1.

For storage and coleslaw: Hidena F_1.

RED CABBAGE

Sow outside in March and April for a summer and autumn crop. Lift any surplus heads before heavy frost and store for winter use.

Sow very thinly, or in soil blocks, in cold frames in September, for planting out in spring for an early summer crop.

Cultivation and nutrient requirements are the same as for summer cabbages.

CABBAGE TYPES

Round summer cabbage: Stonehead.

Pointed summer cabbage: Hispi.

Winter cabbage: January King.

Winter cabbage × Savoy: Celtic.

Recommended cultivars
Langedijk Red Medium, Ruby Ball F_1.

ABYSSINIAN CABBAGE 'KARATE'

This looks like young cabbage plants, growing up to about 2 feet high (60 cm). It is best used as spring greens or a late summer catch crop and cut when between 4 and 10 inches high (10–25 cm). The crop can be cut over several times, starting about 30 to 40 days after sowing, as it grows so rapidly.

Sow in cold frames or under cloches in February for the earliest crop; or outdoors from March onwards. It can also be sown under cover in October, to overwinter as seedlings for a very early crop the following spring. Sow direct in rows no more than 6 inches apart (15 cm), at 3 inches apart (7.5 cm) in the rows.

Dutch white cabbage: Minicole.

Savoy: Ice Queen.

Winter cabbage: Christmas Drumhead.

Spring greens: Abyssinian cabbage.

Calabrese

Calabrese, or Italian sprouting broccoli, is a fast-growing summer vegetable, often ready 80 to 90 days after sowing, producing first a central head, followed by secondary side shoots or spears. The plants are dwarfer than the purple or white sprouting broccoli, rarely more than 2 feet high (60 cm).

Site/soil

See *Brassicas, General*. Calabrese has lower nutrient requirements than many brassicas (see p. 11).

Cultivation

Unlike most brassicas, calabrese is best sown direct rather than being transplanted, because the shock of transplanting encourages the premature production of very small heads. Sow two or three seeds together, thinning to one per site when the seedlings have appeared. The first sowings are made in April or May, with successional sowings in June and July.

Where direct sowing is impossible, sow in pots or soil blocks, planting out carefully in moist soil. This method will also produce a very early crop.

Calabrese is remarkably insensitive to planting distances, but the highest yields of good shoots are obtained from planting at a density of 2 per sq. foot (21/m^2). An average planting arrangement would be 6 inches apart (15 cm) in rows 12 inches apart (30 cm). Closer spacing suppresses the side shoots and gives small terminal spears, which tend all to be ready at the same time. This is useful if the crop is grown for freezing.

Calabrese needs to be watered as frequently as possible in dry weather, up to 4 gal./sq. yd (22 litres/m^2) per week. Where resources are limited, a single heavy watering 2 to 3 weeks before harvest is the most beneficial.

Harvesting

The calabrese season is between June and September, though picking can often continue until plants are damaged by frost. First cut the central head, which can be up to 6 inches in diameter (15 cm). This stimulates the development of side shoots. Early crops may give 3 pickings during the season.

Pests

Calabrese are subject to the usual brassica pests. See pp. i–viii. Caterpillars are a particular nuisance as they conceal themselves inside the heads (see pp. i, v). Mealy aphids may also be a problem (p. iv).

Recommended cultivars

Early: Express Corona F_1, Green Comet F_1.
Mid season: Corvet F_1, Green Duke F_1, El Centro (very dwarf), Premium Crop F_1.

CALABRESE

The central head of a calabrese ready for cutting.

Secondary heads produced about three weeks later.

Cauliflower

Using appropriate varieties, heading at different seasons, cauliflower can be available in the British Isles for most of the year except December and January. Some cauliflower cultivars can grow very large, nearly 3 feet across (90 cm), and may be in the ground for 12 months. Where space is limited the early summer cultivars and mini-cauliflowers are the most suitable.

Site/soil

See *Brassicas, General*. It is essential that cauliflower is grown in deeply dug, fertile, moisture-retentive soil. The key to success is keeping the soil moist during the growing season, and preventing checks of any kind, which lead to poor-quality curds and small premature curds known as buttons.

Cauliflowers do not need a great deal of nitrogenous fertilizer, so that the balance between leaf and curd growth is maintained. A dressing of 4 to 5 oz of Growmore/sq. yd (100–130 g/m^2) before planting will be adequate (for equivalents see p. 11). Cauliflowers prefer a more alkaline soil than most brassicas, in the region of pH 6.5 to 7.5. On very acid soils they may suffer from boron deficiency, and molybdenum deficiency, which causes the malformation 'whiptail' when the growing point fails to develop.

Cultivation

See *Brassicas, General*. Young plants are particularly susceptible to being checked at transplanting, so should be transplanted as young as possible, at about 6 weeks old. For the same reason cauliflowers, though normally transplanted, can be sown direct if space is available, thinning to the spacing required. Spacing varies according to the season of cutting. As a general rule, the later the planting, the wider the spacing can be. For cauliflowers maturing in summer and autumn, spacing will also depend on the amount of watering that can be given if needed.

The recommendations for watering are the same as for other brassicas (p. 35). Lack of water, particularly in the early stages of growth, often results in poor and deformed heads.

The mature curds of cauliflowers which head during winter and early spring may be damaged by severe frost, especially if allowed to thaw out rapidly. This can be prevented by leaning the cauliflower over towards the north, and earthing it up on the south side. In summer curds which are nearly ready can be protected from the sun by bending a large leaf over the top. Bracteated curds, where leaves show between the 'flower' heads, are caused by temperature variations at curd initiation. It is important that winter heading cauliflower should be transplanted in late July or early August to avoid the fault.

The principal sowing and planting dates and suitable cultivars for the main groups are listed below. There is some overlapping between the groups, but as far as possible, cultivars are listed in order of maturity.

Early summer cauliflower: for cutting June/early July. Sow in a cold frame in the first week in October. Prick out into pots (or thin to one per block if sown in soil blocks), and overwinter the seedlings in unheated frames. Plant out in early to mid March as soon as soil conditions are suitable, at 21 inches apart each way (53 cm).
Suitable cultivars: Nevada, Mechelse Classic, Mechelse Delta, Dominant, Snow Crown F_1.

Late summer: for cutting mid July to mid September. Sow in a cold frame in March for the July/early August crop. Sow in late April outdoors for the August/September crop. Plant out at 21 inches apart each way (53 cm). Take great care with watering.
Suitable cultivars: Nevada, Dok (Elgon).

Autumn: for cutting mid-September to December. Sow outdoors in a sheltered part of the garden in mid-May (sowing any earlier can result in faulty curds). Plant out in early July, at 24 inches apart (60 cm) each way.
Suitable cultivars: Wallaby, Flora Blanca Torina, Coolabah, Kangaroo, South Pacific, Barrier Reef.

Winter heading: for cutting December to April.
These are only suitable for growing in the coastal areas of the south, south-west and Wales. Sow early May, transplant late July about 27 inches apart (68 cm) each way.
Suitable cultivars: St Agnes, St David, St Buryan, St Keverne.

Overwintered spring heading: for cutting March to May.
These are unsuitable for the maritime areas of the south and west. Sow in late May, transplanting in mid to late July to about 30 inches apart each way (75 cm). These plants need to be grown 'hard', so

only a little, if any, nitrogen should be applied at the time of planting. A top-dressing in January or February of a nitrogen fertilizer is, however, beneficial (see p. 11).
Suitable cultivars: Angers No. 2, Westmarsh Early and the following Walcheren Winter selections: Armado April, Markanta, Birchington, Armado Tardo.

The purple-headed cauliflower, which has an excellent flavour, also falls in this group. Recommended cultivar: Purple Cape.

Mini-cauliflowers

When early summer cauliflowers are sown close together where they are to mature at 4 plants per sq. foot (43/m^2), they produce a high yield of small heads. These are only $1\frac{1}{2}$ to 3 inches diameter (4–7 cm), each suitable for one portion. The advantage in the garden is that these occupy the ground for a shorter period than large headed cauliflowers, and in the kitchen they are easy to prepare, especially for the freezer. The disadvantage is that all the heads mature over a few days. Sowing small batches in succession during the summer or sowing cultivars of differing maturity at the same time, will overcome this.

Sow at 4 inches apart (10 cm), in rows 9 inches apart (22 cm); or at equidistant spacing, 6 inches apart each way (15 cm). Using early summer cultivars several sowings can be made in succession from April to early July. It may be necessary to water the seedlings to help them to get established, but watering later is only necessary in dry weather.

Suitable cultivars: Garant, Predominant.

CAULIFLOWERS

Heeling over an almost mature cauliflower to the north, for protection from frost.

Mini-cauliflowers are grown close together at 4 plants per square foot.

Kales

Protection of the curd in summer by covering with leaves.

Bracteated curds are caused by fluctuating temperatures.

Kales are the hardiest of all our vegetables, surviving even very severe winters, and breaking into new growth early in spring. With both curly kales (borecole) and the broader, smooth-leaved kales the young shoots are eaten: the leaves of curly kales are also eaten. The season extends from November to April, but kale is most useful in the early months of the year, when fresh vegetables are in short supply. Unfortunately many of the older types of kale are now no longer available.

Site/soil

Kale will tolerate poorer, less prepared soil than most brassicas, but it does best in rich well-cultivated soil, manured the previous autumn. A top-dressing of a nitrogen fertilizer in spring encourages side shoots (see p. 11).

Cultivation

Sow from late April to May or early June, transplanting firmly in July and early August. The dwarfer forms can be planted $1\frac{1}{2}$ feet apart each way (45 cm); taller forms 2 to $2\frac{1}{2}$ feet apart each way (75 cm).

BROAD-LEAVED KALE

The young shoots of a broad-leaved kale, produced in spring.

Kale can also be grown at a closer spacing for an early crop of spring greens. Sow broadcast under cloches in January or February, or outdoors in March and early April, aiming for a spacing of 3 to 4 inches apart (7–10 cm). Cut the plants when no more than 6 inches high (15 cm), leaving the stems to re-sprout.

Harvesting

Pick the young leaves and shoots of the curly kales, taking care not to strip any one plant. Snap off the young shoots of the broad-leaved kales in spring.

Pests and diseases

See *Brassicas, General*. Kale has an advantage over other brassicas in being less susceptible to clubroot, and it is rarely attacked by pigeons.

Recommended cultivars

Dwarf Green Curled (18 inches – 45 cm); Frosty (12 inches – 30 cm); Tall Green/Scotch Curled ($2\frac{1}{2}$ to 3 feet – 75–90 cm); Pentland Brig (2 feet – 60 cm); Fribor F_1 (18 inches – 45 cm).

CURLY KALE

Picking Scotch curly kale: leaves and shoots can be eaten.

Carrots

There are several different types of carrot varieties, classified according to maturity, size and shape. Root shape and colour can, however, be affected by soil and growing conditions. Early cultivars mature relatively quickly and are used when ready. Maincrop cultivars take longer to mature and are used fresh and stored for use during the winter.

The following are the main types of carrots suitable for amateur use, given in order of maturity. In each group there are various selections, claimed to be improvements on the original type.

Amsterdam: Small, slender carrots with cylindrical, stump-shaped roots and smooth skins. Used for early crops and forcing.

Nantes: Cylindrical stump-rooted carrots similar to the Amsterdam type, but slightly broader and longer. Used for early crops and forcing.

Chantenay: Medium sized roots, broader and shorter than Nantes, stump rooted but conical rather than cylindrical in shape. This maincrop type is widely grown for summer use.

Berlicum: Large, late-maturing carrots, cylindrical and stump rooted: very much the same shape as Amsterdam but longer and of better quality. Used for winter storage.

Autumn King: Very long, very large, late-maturing carrots, stump rooted but slightly tapering in shape. These need a long period of growth. Used for winter storage.

Site/soil

Early sowings require a warm sheltered position; later sowings will do in a more open site. Carrots grow best on rich, well-drained, light soils such as coarse sands or friable loams, rather than heavy clay soils. The roots cannot expand in a soil which goes hard when dry. Good soil structure should be encouraged by preparing the soil thoroughly the previous autumn, working in plenty of organic matter. Freshly manured soils should be avoided as they tend to cause root fanging. Carrots prefer a soil pH in the range of 6.5 to 7.5, i.e. slightly acid to slightly alkaline.

Cultivation

Carrots are sown where they are to mature. They

lend themselves to being grown in fairly close rows on the 'bed' system. In preparing the seedbed aim to produce a very fine tilth without consolidating the soil – so that the fingers can be pushed right into the soil when the preparation is complete. Work from paths where possible.

Ideally prepare the seedbed 2 or 3 weeks before sowing, so that the first flush of weeds will germinate and can be hoed off. Nitrogen requirements are low and can be supplied by working $\frac{1}{2}$ oz of Nitrochalk/sq. yd (15 g/m^2) into the seedbed before sowing. For equivalents see p. 11.

Another pre-sowing treatment that is worthwhile will help to protect the seedlings from the frequent pest, carrot root fly. Incorporate an insecticide such as bromophos, chlorpyrifos or diazinon into the seedbed at $\frac{1}{2}$ oz/sq. yd (15 g/m^2) before sowing.

Sow the seed $\frac{1}{2}$ to $\frac{3}{4}$ inch deep (2 cm), as thinly as possible. As it is fairly small it can be mixed with peat, sand, or used and re-dried tea leaves to facilitate even distribution.

Early sowings can be sown more thickly than later sowings as only half the seeds are likely to germinate. The fluid sowing technique is useful for early sowings (see pp. 24–5).

The main sowings are as follows:

For June and July crops
Make the first sowings in frames or under cloches in February or March. The first outdoor sowings can be made in a warm position in February in mild areas, but in colder areas wait until March. Amsterdam and Nantes types are suitable. There are also small round types used for early sowings. Carrot germination is poor in cold soils (below 45 °F – 7 °C), so warm the soil beforehand with cloches if possible, or use fluid sowing to enable the seedlings to get a good start. There is likely to be some bolting with these early crops.

For August and September crops
Sow in March to early April outdoors, using early and Chantenay types.

For October and November crops
Sow outdoors in late April and May, using Chantenay and late types.

For December crops
Sow in late May using Autumn King types.

Cultivation
Modern research aimed at obtaining the highest total usable yields, suggests closer spacings than those traditionally recommended. Some carrots always grow large at the expense of others, so that when high overall yields are obtained, a proportion will be too small for use, though they will be compensated by the weight of the larger carrots.

Carrots are best grown in rows 6 inches apart (15 cm). Sow early cultivars to get plants at 4 inches

CARROT VARIETIES

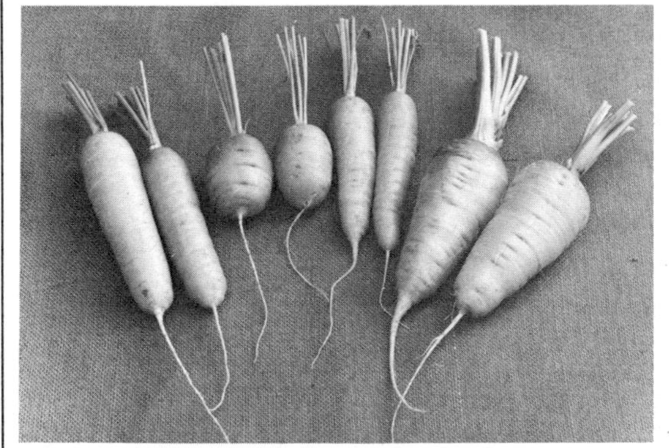

Early: Left to right, Nantes, Paris Market, Amsterdam Forcing, Champion Scarlet Horn.

Maincrop: Left to right, New Red Intermediate, Chantenay, Autumn King.

apart (10 cm) in the rows; this is to to minimize competition and encourage very rapid growth. Sow maincrop cultivars to get plants at 1½ inches apart (4 cm) if medium sized carrots are required; for larger carrots a wider spacing is needed.

Carrots should be thinned as little as possible because the smell of damaged plants attracts the carrot's main pest, root fly. If thinning is necessary do it in the evening, preferably on still, overcast or showery days; water drills before and after thinning; firm the soil around the base of the plant after thinning; and finally remove the thinnings and bury them in the compost heap.

Where carrots are grown in rows 6 inches apart (15 cm), weed them by hand until the plants have two true (feathery) leaves. After this the natural canopy of foliage will virtually suppress further weed growth. If carrots are grown further apart the canopy is slower to suppress weeds and the crop will have to be hoed.

Too much water for carrots encourages the growth of leaves rather than roots. However, root quality will be poor if the soil dries out. In dry weather, watering every two or three weeks will keep the crop growing regularly; about 3 to 4 gal./sq. yd (16–22 litres/m^2) is usually sufficient. In a mature crop root splitting is caused by watering or heavy rainfall after a prolonged dry spell, so maintaining a good supply of soil moisture is an insurance against this.

Harvesting

On light soils early crops of carrots can be pulled as required for use; on heavy soils they may need to be loosened with a fork. The longer maincrop carrots are left in the soil, the higher the yield.

For winter use carrots can either be lifted and stored or left in the soil. The flavour is best if left in the soil, but this is only advisable in light, well-drained soils and if carrot root fly has been controlled. If leaving them in the ground cut off the tops in late November, sprinkle the soil with slug bait, and cover the soil with a layer of leaves or straw about a foot deep (30 cm). Carrots are not generally damaged by the first light frost.

Roots for storage can be lifted from October to December. Cut off the tops at about ½ inch above the crown (1 cm). Reject any diseased or twisted roots, and any with carrot fly damage. Store them in clamps outdoors or boxes indoors. Inspect stored carrots periodically and remove any rotting ones.

CARROTS

Thinning carrots: it is preferable to sow thinly so that there is little need for thinning.

Lifting the roots and removing the tops before storage.

Pests and diseases

Carrot fly is the most damaging pest (see pp. i, v). No measures are totally effective; however, there are several hatches a year, and the risks are lessened if early carrots are lifted by the end of August, and maincrop sowings delayed until the end of May.

Carrot willow aphid may attack seedlings. Spray with an aphicide if noticed.

Young carrots grown on the bed system: see p. 5 for picture of a mature bed.

Storage in boxes with a moist sand filling.

Recommended cultivars
Amsterdam Colora, Amsterdam Forcing, Nantes Tip Top, Chantenay Red Cored, Chantenay Red Cored Royal Chantenay, Berlicum-Berjo, Autumn King-Vita Longa.
Round cultivar: Paris Market-Rondo.

Celeriac

Celeriac is grown primarily for the rather knobbly swollen bulb at the base of the stem, which can grow to 5 inches in diameter (18 cm). Celeriac is a useful alternative for celery, being hardier, less prone to pests and diseases, and easier to grow.

Site/soil
By nature a marshland plant, celeriac requires fertile, moisture-retentive soil, rich in organic matter. It can be grown in damper parts of the garden, and will tolerate light shade.

Cultivation
Celeriac must have a long unchecked, growing season, and adequate moisture throughout the growing season if it is to grow to a worthwhile size. Start growing it early, sowing if possible in February or March in gentle heat in seed boxes or several seeds per pot or soil block, or sow in March/April in a cold frame. Germination is often erratic.

Prick out the seedlings when large enough to handle, or thin to one per soil block. Harden them off gradually before planting outside in May, at 12 to 15 inches apart each way (30–37 cm), in shallow drills, taking care not to bury the crowns.

Celeriac needs ample water throughout the summer, so water the plants if rainfall is short. Remove the outer leaves at the end of July to expose the crown. Mulching is usually beneficial.

Harvesting
Celeriac is ready from October until April or May the following year. The roots tend to deteriorate if lifted, so are best left in the ground in winter, protected from severe frosts with a layer of bracken or straw 6 inches thick (15 cm), tucked around the plants. Alternatively they can be lifted for convenience and stored in boxes indoors, leaving on the central tuft of leaves.

If the ground in which they are growing is required in spring, they can be lifted and temporarily heeled in until used.

Pests and diseases
Celeriac is subject to celery fly (see p. vi), but this is rarely serious. Blistered leaflets can be picked off by hand.

Recommended cultivar
Marble Ball.

CELERIAC

Planting pot-raised plants in a sunken drill.

Removing the outer leaves at the end of July to expose the crown.

Protecting the crowns from frost by tucking straw around the plants.

Celery

The traditional English 'trench' celery is grown for its blanched leaf stalks, used mainly around Christmas. It requires considerable space and skill to grow well. The more easily grown 'self-blanching' celery is less hardy, and doesn't form the huge distinctly flavoured stalks of trench celery, but can be grown on the flat, and forms a practical alternative for use in summer and autumn. Both types are descended from a marsh plant and will benefit from moisture during growth.

SELF-BLANCHING CELERY

Most of the self-blanching cultivars have off-white or yellowish stalks, which can be rendered whiter by planting relatively close, so partially excluding light. The green-stalked American Green types are eaten green.

Site/soil

Celery requires an open site and very fertile, moisture-retentive but well-drained soil, rich in organic matter. It does not grow well in an acid soil, one with a pH about 6.6 or slightly above is best.

Cultivation

Celery needs to be grown steadily without any growth check such as a sudden temperature change or a shortage of water. Either check to growth may induce bolting or the production of stringy stems.

If available use thiram-treated seed as a precaution against leaf spot infection. Sow seeds in gentle heat in seed trays or in soil blocks no earlier than the third week of March or into April. Celery germinates best at soil temperatures between 50 and 60 °F (10–15 °C). Sow on the surface or very shallowly, as celery only germinates in the light. Try to maintain an even temperature after germination: if seedlings are subjected to temperatures below 50 °F (10 °C) for more than 12 hours the mature plants are liable to bolt. (If these conditions are difficult to fulfil it will be better to buy in plants.) Celery is a good subject for fluid sowing, which results in an improved germination percentage (see pp. 24–5).

Prick out the seedlings when they are large enough to handle, or thin to one per soil block. Raising celery in soil blocks or small pots helps to minimize the shock of transplanting. Plants must be hardened off very carefully before planting out, to prevent bolting.

Celery has a high requirement for nitrogen

during growth, and will benefit from fertilizer incorporated into the soil before transplanting (see p. 11). Plant in frames in early to mid-May, or outside after all danger of frost is past, at the end of May or early June. Reject any plants with blistered leaves, as these will be infected with celery fly. Plants are ready for transplanting when they have 5 or 6 true leaves.

Celery should be planted in a block formation to encourage the self-blanching process. (The ground can be marked out in squares beforehand.) Plant so that the crown is at soil level. There is a choice of spacings, as follows: a maximum of 11 inches apart each way (28 cm) gives high yields with good blanching of the sticks. Spacing 6 inches apart (15 cm) each way gives a higher total yield of smaller sticks with slender, good-quality hearts, but this close spacing is expensive if plants are bought. Spacing at 9 inches apart (22 cm) each way is a compromise. Once the plants are established, straw can be tucked around those on the outside of the block to assist in blanching.

Celery needs to be watered generously during its growing period to obtain the best size and quality of stems; up to 4 gal./sq. yd/week (22 litres/m^2) in dry weather. A top-dressing of nitrogenous fertilizer (sodium nitrate is particularly suitable for celery) can be applied about 4 to 6 weeks after transplanting (see p. 11).

Harvesting

Self-blanching celery is ready for cutting from about the end of July, continuing until the frosts. It may be necessary to discard some of the outer stalks.

Pests and diseases

Celery fly or celery leaf miner is the most serious pest (see p. vi). If possible avoid planting near parsnips, which may also be affected.

Slugs are a very serious problem with celery, and preventive measures should be taken as soon as celery is planted out (see p. iv).

Recommended cultivars

Avonpearl, Golden Self Blanching (these are liable to bolt if sown too early), Lathom Self Blanching (good resistance to bolting).

American green cultivars are Greensnap, Tendercrisp.

TRENCH CELERY

There are white, pink and red stemmed cultivars of trench celery. The stems are blanched by planting the celery in a trench and earthing up the stems as the plant grows. It is one of the more difficult vegetables to grow well.

Site/soil

A sunny open site is necessary. Fertile soil

CELERY

Trench celery being cleaned and tied before earthing up.

An alternative to earthing up for celery on the flat is to tie paper cylinders around the stems.

SELF-BLANCHING CELERY

Planting the young plants at 9 inches apart in a block, guided by marked squares.

Lifting in mid-September: the straw has helped to blanch the outside row.

TYPES OF STICK CELERY

Left to right, Greensnap, Golden Self-Blanching, Green Pascal.

containing plenty of organic matter is essential. To achieve this dig out a trench 15 inches wide (40 cm) and 12 inches deep (30 cm) preferably in the autumn before the crop is to be grown, and work a thick layer of manure or compost into the bottom of the trench. The soil is then returned to the trench, to within 3 to 4 inches of ground level (10 cm), leaving the remainder alongside for subsequent earthing up.

Cultivation

Sow the seeds in heat (50–66 °F – 10–19 °C) in March, remembering that celery seeds need light for the best germination. Prick out and harden off the seedlings, before planting out in late May or June.

Earthing up is easiest if the celery is planted in single rows with 9 inches between plants (22 cm). However, somewhat wider trenches can be made, and celery planted in a staggered double row, with the plants about 10 inches apart (23 cm). Plant in moist soil and water well after planting. Water subsequently as for self-blanching celery.

Start earthing up when the plants are about 12 inches tall (30 cm), usually about mid-August. Before earthing up, tie the stems loosely just below the leaves, remove any suckers, and water the soil so that it is moist. Draw the soil up about 3 inches around the plants (7 cm). Repeat this operation twice more at intervals of about 3 weeks until only the tops of the plants are exposed. Never earth up higher than the base of the green leaves, and take care not to let any soil fall into the heart of the plant.

When grown on the flat, brown paper or black polythene can be tied around the stems in stages, securely fastened with raffia, covering 3 to 4 inches at a time (8–10 cm).

In late winter place bracken or other protective material over the plants, so that they will remain in good condition, protected from heavy frost, as long as possible.

Harvesting

Lifting usually starts in November, using the white cultivars first until about Christmas. The pink and red varieties are slightly hardier and can be used later.

Pests and diseases

See self-blanching celery (p. 87).

Recommended cultivars

Giant White, Giant Pink (Clayworth Prize Pink).

Chicories

WITLOOF CHICORY

Witloof chicory is a hardy vegetable, very much like dandelion in appearance. It is grown for the conical white heads of leaves, obtained by forcing the roots in the dark in winter after lifting them from the open ground. This blanching process removes their bitterness. Chicory has a distinct flavour, and is an excellent winter vegetable.

Site/soil

Chicory should be grown in an open site. The soil needs to be fertile, but not freshly manured or the roots are liable to be forked.

Cultivation

Sow in rows 12 inches apart (30 cm) in May or early June. Sow thinly as the germination rates are very high, aiming to get plants at 6 inches apart (15 cm). During the summer keep the plants weeded, and water to prevent the soil drying out. Leave the plants growing until late autumn.

Forcing in the garden

This is feasible in light or sandy soils. The heads are ready later than those forced indoors, but the flavour is said to be better. In late October or early November cut the leaves off the plant at about an inch (2.5 cm) above the neck. Earth up the roots so they are covered with 6 to 7 inches of soil (15–17 cm). This ridge can be covered with straw or cloches to bring the heads on more quickly. The heads will slowly force their way through the soil, and will be ready for cutting between January and March, depending on temperature.

Forcing indoors

Roots are lifted any time between late October and December, and any which are fanged or very thin discarded. The ideal size for forcing is between 1¼ and 2 inches in diameter across the top (4–5 cm); smaller roots make an insignificant head, and larger roots a very loose head. Trim the leaves off at an inch (2.5 cm) above the neck. If the weather has been mild stack the roots in a heap outside for two or three weeks, as exposure to cold is necessary to break their dormancy. Then dry them off, and store them until required for forcing either flat in boxes in a shed, covered with sand to prevent them drying out, or outside covered with straw.

For a regular supply of heads between December and April it is best to force a few roots at a time.

WITLOOF CHICORY

A mature row in summer; plants at 5 to 6 inches apart.

Forcing in situ*: the tops are cut off and plants earthed up in early winter.*

Forcing indoors: lifted trimmed roots can be planted in a flower pot; the right-hand pot is used as a cover (with the drainage holes blocked) to create darkness.

Well-grown heads, ready for cutting.

They need to be forced in total darkness with a little warmth. The temperature can be between 50 and 65 °F (10–18 °C), but the lower the temperature the longer it takes. At 64 °F heads are generally ready in 3 weeks.

The simplest method is to plant 3 to 4 roots together in moist soil in an 8 or 9 inch flower pot (20 cm). The roots can be trimmed to a length of 7 to 8 inches (20 cm) if necessary. Invert another pot of the same size over the first, blocking the drainage holes to keep out the light. Put the pots in an airing cupboard, or other suitable place for forcing.

Alternatively roots can be planted in a box, in the soil under greenhouse staging, or in a cold frame, devising some method of excluding light, such as black polythene. Light can also be excluded by covering the roots with an 8 inch layer (20 cm) of soil, sand, leaf mould, or any material through which the heads can gradually force their way. (Tighter heads are formed where a solid covering such as this is used, but the flavour is indistinguishable from those forced in pots or under black polythene; see also Recommended cultivars.) Water the roots if the soil is becoming dry.

Harvesting

The heads are ready when the tips are visible through the soil. Cut them when they seem to be a reasonable size with a sharp knife an inch or so above the neck, as the roots sometimes re-sprout to give a second, smaller head. Keep the heads covered or in a dark place until required, as they become green and bitter on exposure to light.

Recommended cultivars

Witloof or Belgian (traditional).
Crispa, Normato are newer cultivars which make tight heads without a soil covering.

SUGAR LOAF CHICORY

This type of chicory, somewhat like a cos lettuce in appearance, has a head of leaves so tightly packed that they blanch themselves. It makes a crisp, slightly tart salad in late autumn. The older varieties were generally lifted whole in late autumn and stored. Modern cultivars withstand lower temperatures, frequently surviving the winter if cloched.

Cultivation

Sow in fertile, moisture-retentive soil, in June or July, in rows 12 inches apart (30 cm). Aim to space the plants at 10 inches apart (25 cm). Keep the plants well watered during the summer, and they will form good heads by autumn. Protect them with cloches before the onset of severe weather, or cover them loosely with bracken or straw, held in place with wire hoops.

Harvesting

Cut the heads, leaving the stump in the soil, as it will often re-sprout to give useful salad leaves early in spring. Traditionally sugar loaf chicory was stored in frost-proof sheds or cellars, or in circular heaps outdoors, about 3 feet high (90 cm), made with the heads pointing to the centre, and covered with straw.

Recommended cultivars

Sugar Loaf (Pain de Sucre): traditional.
Crystal Head, Snowflake, Winter Fare: modern.

RED CHICORY

Many chicories are grown on the Continent which are green in summer, becoming red and variegated in winter. They are of varying degrees of hardiness. Red Verona is the best known in this country. Cultivate as for sugar loaf chicory. In the autumn it can either be lifted and forced as for Witloof chicory, or left in the ground, where it will often form dense, ball-shaped heads of leaves which can be cut in winter. The plants can be protected with a light covering of bracken, but cloche protection is inadvisable, as it tends to encourage rotting.

SUGAR LOAF CHICORY

Mature plant: the section shows the crisp naturally blanched inner leaf.

Chinese Cabbage

There are many types of Chinese cabbage, but the typical one grown in this country has a long barrel-shaped head of tightly folded leaves. The leaves are distinguished by a broad white midrib (which is edible) and prominent white veins. It is a fast growing brassica, a semi-tropical crop, needing plenty of water and nitrogen.

Site/soil
Chinese cabbage needs an open site, though it will tolerate light shade. It does best on fertile, moisture-retentive soils, which should be limed if acid. It is a useful crop to follow early potatoes or early peas.

Cultivation
Chinese cabbage is best sown in July or August; being a 'short day' plant, earlier sowings are liable to bolt. It is easily checked by transplanting, so preferably sow direct in rows 18 inches apart (45 cm), thinning to a foot apart (90 cm). Water the drill before sowing if conditions are dry. Alternatively sow in soil blocks or individual pots to minimize any transplanting check.

Water if necessary, giving up to 4 gal./sq. yd (22 litres/m^2) in dry weather. Encourage rapid growth by keeping the plants weeded and mulched. For fertilizers see p. 11.

Most varieties of Chinese cabbage only tolerate light frost, but outdoor plants can be protected in late autumn with cloches or low polythene tunnels to improve their quality and prolong their usefulness.

Harvesting
Heads are often ready 9 or 10 weeks after sowing. The main season is September to November. Cut the heads at ground level, leaving the stumps to re-sprout. If wrapped in polythene the heads can be kept several weeks in a refrigerator. They are easily revived in cold water if they have wilted.

Pests and disease
The most common problems are those of other brassicas, viz. slugs (see p. iv), cabbage root fly (pp. i, v) and clubroot (pp. i, vii). Rotate Chinese cabbage as for other brassicas.

Some recommended cultivars
Nagaoka 50 Days F_1, Tip Top F_1.

COURGETTES See Marrows, p. 102.

CHINESE CABBAGE

A young crop of the hearted type.

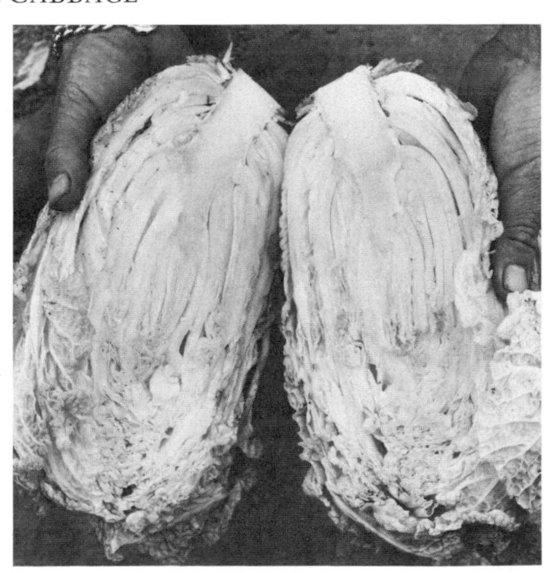

A mature head in October, 14 weeks after sowing.

Cucumbers

The main types of cucumber are the long, smooth greenhouse or frame cucumber, the shorter, prickly skinned but much hardier ridge or outdoor cucumber; and the smaller gherkins used for pickling. Greenhouse cucumbers are a specialized crop requiring considerable heat to be grown successfully. Only ridge cucumbers and gherkins will be covered here.

Some excellent new cultivars of outdoor cucumbers have been bred in recent years. They are often over 12 inches long (30 cm), and have high levels of tolerance to disease and low temperatures. These and other ridge cucumbers can be grown successfully both outdoors and in frames. No cucumber, however, will tolerate frost.

Site/soil

A sunny sheltered site is required; cucumbers tolerate light shade in summer. They can also be grown in 10 inch (25 cm) pots or growing bags. The outdoor crop always benefits from cloche or similar protection in the early stages of growth.

Cucumbers require very fertile and moisture-retentive soil, rich in organic matter, and slightly acid to neutral. Prepare individual holes for each cucumber, about a foot deep (30 cm) and 1½ feet wide (45 cm). Work plenty of very well-rotted manure, compost or rotted straw into the hole, and cover it with 6 to 8 inches of soil (15–18 cm) to make a slightly raised mound on which the cucumbers are sown or planted. This ensures good drainage and so helps to avoid the root rots to which cucumbers are prone.

Cultivation

Ridge cucumbers can either be grown flat on the ground or, preferably, trained to some support such as a trellis or wire netting. The Japanese cultivars can be trained successfully on tripods of canes. Gherkins are usually grown on the flat.

Cucumbers are adversely affected by transplanting, so it is best to sow them in their cropping position, or to raise plants in small pots or soil blocks to minimize the transplanting shock. Do not sow outdoors until mid-May (south) or end of May (north), as seeds will not germinate at temperatures below 56 °F (23 °C). Sow ¾ to 1 inch deep (2–2.5 cm). If sowing outdoors sow 2 or 3 seeds per site, thinning to one after germination. Cover with individual jam jars or cloches after sowing.

Alternatively sow indoors in gentle heat in April, planting outside when danger of frost is past, usually about the end of May. Cucumbers are normally ready for planting 4 to 5 weeks after sowing.

Cucumbers can be planted 1½ feet apart (45 cm) where grown to climb, and 2 to 2½ feet apart (60–75 cm) if grown on the flat. Water well after planting. Lay straw around the plants grown on the flat to

OUTDOOR CUCUMBERS

Planting out a cucumber on a prepared mound.

Ridge cucumbers being trained up wire netting support.

keep the fruits clean or use a plastic film mulch.

Cucumbers require plenty of water, especially once they have started flowering and the fruits are setting and growing. Pinch out the tops of the plants when they reach the top of the support; growth will continue on laterals arising from the main stem. It is not necessary to remove the male flowers with ridge cucumbers to prevent the fruit being fertilized and becoming bitter, as is the case with the traditional greenhouse varieties.

Harvesting

The outdoor crop is ready between July and September. Keep picking the fruits once they have reached a reasonable size, to encourage further production.

Pests and diseases

The most serious pest outdoors is aphids (see p. iv). The most common diseases are cucumber mosaic virus (pp. ii, viii) and powdery mildew (p. vii). See also root rots (p. 93).

Some recommended cultivars

Japanese: Burpless Tasty Green F_1; Burpee Hybrid.
Traditional: Perfection.

CUCUMBER TYPES

Left to right, long greenhouse type, ridge and gherkin cucumbers.

Endive

Endives are lettuce-like plants which are widely grown on the Continent. There are two distinct types: curled endive, which has very finely divided frilly leaves, and the usually broad-leaved Batavian endive, which is hardier. Both are rather bitter to taste, and blanching them before use will make them sweeter. This is less necessary with some of the modern cultivars which have a larger inner core of white leaves. Endive is particularly useful in late summer, winter and early spring when lettuce is scarce.

Site/soil

Endive requires an open situation and fertile, moisture-retentive soil. Early summer sowings can be made in light shade.

Cultivation

Endive seed can be sown direct or seedlings transplanted. Space curled types at 12 inches apart (30 cm), and broad-leaved types 15 inches apart (38 cm). Transplant thinnings to give a successive crop. The main sowing dates are:
April (both types) for a summer crop.
June and July (both types) for autumn and early winter use.

ENDIVE

Curled type tied with raffia for partial blanching.

August (broad-leaved) for late winter use. Sow outdoors, but cover with cloches in October. This crop can either be allowed to form a full head, or used as a cut-and-come-again crop, cutting the leaves when about 4 or 5 inches high (10 cm), and allowing them to re-sprout during the winter and early spring.

September and October (broad-leaved) for a crop the following April and May. Sow indoors and overwinter the seedlings under cover. Transplant outdoors in very early spring.

Blanching

Plants are blanched when nearly full grown, about 2 to 3 months after planting. Blanch a few plants at a time, as they deteriorate very rapidly after blanching. Do not start blanching unless the leaves are dry, or the plant will rot while covered (if necessary put cloches over the plants a few days beforehand to dry them). Take precautions against slugs.

Blanching in position. Ensure the leaves are dry, then bunch them up and tie them towards the top with raffia. For total blanching cover the plant with an upturned flower pot with the drainage holes blocked to exclude light, or box them around with wooden boards.

Partial blanching is achieved simply by tying the leaves, or by placing a slate or tile over the centre of the plant.

Blanching lifted plants. Preferably lift the plants before the first hard frosts, and plant them close together in a cold frame or under greenhouse staging, or in pots or boxes. Tie the leaves together before blanching, and exclude light by the use of black polythene, by putting pots or boxes in a dark cellar, or by covering the plants with straw or dry leaves. Warm conditions are unnecessary.

Blanching time varies from about a week in warm weather to 3 weeks in midwinter. Use the plants immediately; they become green and bitter fairly rapidly on re-exposure to light.

Pests and diseases

Remarkably few. A spring crop under cover may be attacked by aphids (see p. iv).

Recommended cultivars

Curled: Moss or Green Curled, Pancalière.
Broad-leaved: Batavian Broad Leaved, Golda.

Broad-leaved type being blanched by an upturned plate.

Blanching by covering with a plastic pot (a piece of wood covers the drainage holes).

Florence Fennel

With its feathery foliage, florence or sweet fennel is among the most decorative of garden vegetables. Unlike the perennial herb, the bases of the leaf stalks swell to form a succulent aniseed-flavoured bulb, just above ground level.

Site/soil
Fennel does best on fertile, light, sandy, well-drained soils.

Cultivation
It is not easy to grow first-class fennel in this country, as plants tend to bolt rather than swelling up at the base. Some varieties are very sensitive to day length, and are likely to bolt if sown before mid-June. Secondly, fennel is liable to bolt if its growth is checked, which can be caused by a shortage of water, sudden fluctuations in temperature, or even by being subjected to draughts.

The main sowings are from April to June for the July to September crop, and in July until the first week of August for the October to November crop. Sow direct, or in soil blocks or small pots for planting out. Plant at 12 to 14 inches apart (30–35 cm). Growth is fast in favourable conditions.

Some recommended cultivars
Perfection, Zefo Fino.
Sweet Florence (late sowings only).

FLORENCE FENNEL

In the foreground are lifted and trimmed bulbs: they can be used raw or cooked. The leaves can be used for seasoning.

Kohl Rabi

A curious looking member of the brassica family, the edible part is a ball-like swelling in the stem, at an inch or two above ground level (5 cm). Kohl rabi is often used as a turnip substitute: it withstands drought and heat better and is more resistant to clubroot. There are purple and white or green forms, according to the skin colour.

Site/soil
Kohl rabi does best if grown in fertile, light sandy soils, limed if acid. Rotate as for other brassicas. It makes a useful catch crop, as in rich soil and moist conditions, it can be ready for use 7 weeks after sowing.

Cultivation
For a continuous supply sow small quantities in succession from February (in mild districts) to September. The green forms mature fastest and are generally used for sowings before June. Purple types are later maturing and are sown from June onwards for use in winter.

Sow thinly in drills 12 inches apart (30 cm),

KOHL RABI

Kohl rabi should be lifted for eating when no larger than a ten

aiming to space the plants at 9 inches apart (27 cm). If thinning is necessary it is most important to do it early, so that development is not impeded. Seedlings can be transplanted when no more than 2 inches tall (5 cm). For fertilizer needs see p. 11.

Harvesting

Use kohl rabi when young, between golf-ball and tennis-ball size; larger ones become woody. The plants are fairly hardy and can be left in the ground in winter in most parts of the country. Although quality is lost in storage, they can be stored in sand in boxes (see p. 40), after trimming off the outer leaves, but leaving a central tuft.

Pests and diseases

Flea beetle and cabbage root fly are the most likely pests (see p. v); clubroot the most likely disease (see p. vii).

Cultivars

White or Green Vienna, Purple Vienna.

Leeks

Leeks are one of the most useful of the hardy winter vegetables, their season extending from late summer until late spring the following year. They are grown for the white shank at the base of the leaves, which is to some extent naturally blanched, though further blanching is encouraged by deep planting or earthing up.

Site/soil

An open site is required. Leeks do best in rich, well-worked, light loamy soils, into which plenty of well-rotted manure or compost has been worked. If necessary this can be done shortly before the crop is planted. Preferred pH is slightly acid to slightly alkaline (6.5–7.5).

Leeks have a fibrous root system and help to improve soil structure. Their site should be rotated each year as with onions.

Cultivation

There are early, mid-season, and late cultivars of leeks, maturing approximately September to November, December to February, March to early May respectively. The earlier cultivars tend to be taller, with longer white shafts and paler foliage; later ones are thicker, with a shorter area of blanched stem and darker leaves. They are also hardier. As a general rule, the longer the growing season, and the larger the leek at transplanting, the larger the leek will eventually be.

Soil temperatures of at least 45 °F (7 °C) are necessary for leek seed to germinate well. The very earliest sowings can be made in gentle heat in February, pricking out and hardening off the leeks before planting them out in May. The main sowings outdoors are made in a seedbed from March to early May, provided the soil is warm enough. Early outdoor sowings can also be made under cloches. Sow thinly, in drills $\frac{1}{2}$ to $\frac{3}{4}$ inch deep (2 cm).

The main transplanting season is June, though planting can continue into July and early August as ground becomes available. Water the seedbed thoroughly before lifting the seedlings. The best size for transplanting is when the leeks are about 8 inches tall (20 cm), between 10 and 15 weeks old. The tips of the leaves can be trimmed back slightly to prevent them dragging on the soil after planting.

Leeks have high nitrogen requirements because of their long growing season. They benefit from incorporation of manure in the autumn before planting, and also from a nitrogen fertilizer forked into the soil immediately before planting out (see p. 11).

The highest yields of average-sized leeks are obtained by planting 6 inches apart (15 cm) in rows 12 inches apart (30 cm). Closer spacing will not reduce the total yield, but will give small, more slender leeks.

There are several methods of planting. The first two facilitate blanching by planting relatively deeply, though plants should not be planted so deeply that they are buried. The simplest method is to make holes 5 to 6 inches deep (15 cm) with a dibber, dropping one plant into each hole. The soil will fall back naturally into the hole during the growing season. The second method is to plant in a V-shaped drill, 3 inches deep (7.5 cm), which is subsequently filled in to blanch the stems.

Leeks can also be planted on the flat, though this is generally done only on very shallow or very heavy soils. In all cases, a further area of leaf can be blanched by earthing up several times during growth.

Water in well after transplanting, and if dry weather follows, water daily (about ⅛ pint per plant (70 ml)) until the plants are well established. Additional watering is only necessary if very large leeks are required.

Harvesting

Leeks can be lifted as required, but mid-season and late cultivars are hardy enough to stand outside in winter. If the ground where they are growing is required in late spring they can be lifted and heeled in temporarily in an out-of-the-way corner.

Pests/diseases

Leeks are relatively trouble free, the most serious pest being stem and bulb eelworm (see p. vi). In some seasons leek rust is a troublesome disease (see p. vii).

Some recommended cultivars

(AM=Autumn Mammoth selection)
Early: AM Walton Mammoth.
Mid: AM Argenta, King Richard, Lyon.
Late: AM Goliath, AM Snowstar, Giant Winter-Cataline, Musselburgh, Winter Crop, Yates Empire.

LEEKS

Young leek plants having their tops trimmed before planting, so that they do not drag on the soil.

Watering in the plants to the soil round the roots (see also picture on p. 32).

Lettuce

Several distinct types of lettuce are grown, hearted and non-hearted. Of the hearted lettuces, the round-headed cabbage type includes the soft-leaved 'butterheads', and the crisp-leaved 'crispheads', which are slower to bolt. Cos lettuces are upright, with thicker, long leaves; they normally take longer to mature than cabbage lettuces.

Non-hearting lettuces include the many decorative Salad Bowl types, some with deeply indented leaves. These provide constant picking throughout the summer and are slow to run to seed.

In many parts of the country lettuces can be obtained from early spring until November, with the use of cloches.

Site/soil

Lettuce must have an open site and light, fertile, moisture-retentive soil. Lettuce will not grow well on poor soil which dries out during the summer. The preferred pH range is slightly acid to slightly alkaline. Wherever possible rotate lettuce crops to avoid a build-up of fungus diseases. Ideally the ground should be dug over the previous autumn, working in manure or compost. A base dressing of general fertilizer can be given 10 days before sowing or planting (see p. 11).

The smaller varieties of lettuce, such as Little Gem and Tom Thumb, are useful for intercropping.

Cultivation

Lettuces can be sown from February to October, using suitable cultivars. (Consult current seed catalogues for the optimum sowing time for any variety.) For a continuous supply of butterhead lettuces it is advisable to sow small amounts of seeds every two weeks or so; mature plants will stand for up to 5 or 7 days without bolting. Crisphead types will stand for up to a week longer. Where possible use mosaic tested seed, to lessen the risk of plants being infected with lettuce mosaic virus.

Lettuces can either be sown direct, or in seed trays or soil blocks for transplanting. Unless soil blocks are used, sowings between May and mid-August are best made direct as lettuces are difficult to transplant successfully in hot weather. Sow in drills $\frac{1}{2}$ to $\frac{3}{4}$ inch deep (2 cm).

Lettuces germinate well at low temperatures, but germination is often erratic in summer if soil temperatures are over 77 °F (25 °C), especially during the critical period a few hours after sowing. This is particularly true of butterhead varieties but

LETTUCES

Planting lettuces: care should be taken not to bury the lower leaves.

Thinning lettuces: it is not advisable to transplant lettuces in summer.

Cutting closely sown 'leaf lettuce'. The roots are left to re-sprout to give a second cutting.

less so with crisphead varieties. The problem can be overcome by watering after sowing to reduce the soil temperature, or by sowing between 2 and 4 p.m., so that the critical period falls during the cooler hours of evening and night. Fluid sowing (pp. 24–5) also overcomes the problem as the seeds are past the sensitive stage when sown.

Except in mid-summer, thinnings can be transplanted to give a successive crop maturing approximately 10 days later; but reject any poor seedlings. Plant with the seed leaves just above soil level.

Spacing varies according to the cultivar used, but average recommendations for those grown in spring, autumn and winter, and for small ones such as Little Gem and Tom Thumb, are 9 × 9 inches (25 × 25 cm). Summer plantings can be 12 × 12 inches (30 × 30 cm). Crisphead lettuces need 12 × 15 inches (30 × 37 cm) or 15 × 15 inches (37 × 37 cm) to produce good solid heads.

In dry periods lettuces will need to be watered frequently throughout growth to obtain crops of good size and quality – up to 4 gal./sq. yd/week (22 litres/m^2). If water is in short supply the most effective time to water is 7 to 10 days before maturity.

The main sowing periods for lettuces are given below, though there is in practice considerable overlap between sowings. Appropriate cultivars for the season must be used. See recommended cultivars, opposite.

Early sowings under glass for a late May, early June crop outdoors. Sow mid-February (in the south) or early March (in the north). Sow either direct in a frame or under cloches, or in boxes for transplanting outdoors in a sheltered position, or under cloches, at the end of March or early April.

Main outdoor summer sowings for crops from June to October. Sow from late March to early July, sowing direct from mid-May onwards. These plants can be cloched in autumn to improve their quality.

Protected winter crop to mature in November/December, or February/March the following year. Sow outdoors or indoors, between late August and early October, for planting into a frame in late autumn.

Outdoor overwintering hardy lettuce for a May and June crop. Sow direct at the end of August or early September and thin if necessary to 3 inches apart (8 cm) in October. They overwinter in the open and are thinned to their final spacing (12 × 12 inches: 30 × 30 cm) the following spring to give an early outdoor crop. The crop will be 2 to 3 weeks earlier and of better quality, if protected with cloches during the winter. A nitrogenous top-dressing given in March will encourage growth (see p. 11).

Leaf lettuce

This is a technique for obtaining heavy yields of

LETTUCE TYPES

Cos lettuce.

Crisphead lettuce.

leafy lettuce from a small area. The plants are grown close together, which encourages the formation of leaves rather than hearts. The leaves are cut an inch above ground level (2.5 cm), and the stump left to produce a second crop. This is cut 4 to 7 weeks later, depending on the season. The crop must be grown in fertile, weed-free soil, and kept well watered. It is best sown in rows 5 inches apart (12 cm), aiming to get plants an inch apart (2.5 cm) in the rows.

The following are the NVRS recommendations to give a continuous supply of lettuce leaves from mid-May to mid-October. An area of a square yard sown per week will give ample supplies for an average family.

Make weekly sowings from mid-April to mid-May. These will be ready for the first cut about 7½ weeks later, from late May to the end of June, giving a second cut a further 7½ weeks later, from early July to mid-August.

Make three further sowings weekly in the first 3 weeks in August. These will be ready for the first cut within 3½ weeks, and for the second cut 4½ weeks later, in the first three weeks of October.

Cos lettuce tends to be more suitable than other types for growing as leaf lettuce.

Pests and diseases

The principal pests on lettuces are greenfly and root aphid, and in some areas, cutworm, leatherjackets, slugs, snails and birds (see p. iv). The cultivars Avoncrisp and Avondefiance have a considerable resistance to root aphid and also to some races of downy mildew.

The principal diseases are grey mould (see p. vii), downy mildew (pp. ii, vii), lettuce mosaic virus (p. viii), and in seedlings, damping off (p. vi).

Some recommended cultivars

For early sowings under glass:
Hilde II, Little Gem, Reskia, Tom Thumb, Unrivalled, Winter Density and Salad Bowl types.

Main summer sowings in the open:
Butterhead: Avondefiance, Continuity, Reskia, Tom Thumb.
Cos: Little Gem, Winter Density.
Crisphead: Avoncrisp, Buttercrunch, Great Lakes, Minetto, Webbs Wonderful, Windermere.
Salad Bowl types.

Protected winter crop:
Dandie, Kwiek, Ravel, Unrivalled.

Outdoor hardy overwintering lettuce:
Butterhead types: Imperial Winter, Valdor.
Cos types: Little Gem, Lobjoit's Green, Winter Density.

Leaf lettuce:
Lobjoit's Cos, Paris White Cos.

Salad Bowl.

Butterhead type.

Marrows, Courgettes, Squashes and Pumpkins

Of the immense and varied family of gourds, the marrow (or vegetable marrow as it is sometimes listed) is the most widely grown in this country. In recent years the use of courgettes or zucchini has become popular. These are immature marrows cut when about 4 inches long (10 cm); some varieties of marrows, notably hybrid bush types, are more suitable for use as courgettes than others.

Marrows are generally green or white, but a golden form is also used for courgettes. Plants are either a compact bush form, spreading to about a yard (just under a metre) in diameter, or trailing, with shoots growing several yards long.

Bush types are more practical for most gardens and tend to crop earlier. Trailing types can be trained over fences or strong supports, up tripods of canes or poles, or into a circular form by pinning down the main shoots with pieces of wire or wooden pegs. They are generally grown for the maincrop supply.

In North America gourds are divided into summer squashes, which are used fresh in summer, and winter squashes, which develop tougher skins and can either be used fresh or stored for winter. Summer squashes include the fluted custard pie and patty pan marrows, and crookneck squash. Winter squashes include ordinary and Turk's turban pumpkins, Hubbard, acorn and butternut squash, and the vegetable spaghetti marrow.

All gourds are cultivated like marrows. None of them are hardy.

Site/soil

Marrows like an open sunny site, and very rich, moisture-retentive but well-drained soil, slightly acid to neutral. It is best to prepare individual holes into which plenty of well-rotted organic matter has been worked, as for cucumbers (see p. 93). The practice of growing marrows on manure or compost heaps is not recommended, as it encourages lush leafy growth at the expense of fruit (particularly early in the season); moreover heaps tend to dry out rapidly in hot weather.

Cultivation

Marrows do not germinate at soil temperatures below 56 °F (13 °C), but grow very rapidly in warm conditions, so little is gained by sowing too early. Seed is sown at ¾ to 1 inch deep (2.5 cm).

They can be sown indoors in soil blocks or small pots towards the end of April and will be ready for planting out within 4 to 5 weeks. Harden off well before planting out after all risk of frost is past.

Alternatively sow direct towards the end of May, preferably under cloches or individual jam jars. Sow 2 or 3 seeds per site, thinning to one after germination, leaving the strongest seedling.

Bush types can be grown about 3 feet apart (90 cm), and trailing types about 4 feet apart (1.2 m).

Marrows require a great deal of water. They should be watered lightly after planting so that they are quickly established, and subsequently as frequently as practical throughout growth, up to 2 gal. weekly (11 litres). Water is particularly important when the plants are flowering and as fruits are setting and growing. Mulching the plants will help to conserve moisture in the soil.

Marrows have male and female flowers. (Female flowers are distinguished by the small embryo marrows seen at the base of the flowers.) Sometimes plants produce many male flowers early in the season before any females appear. Flowers are insect

MARROWS

Trailing marrow plants trained up a wigwam of poles.

pollinated, and in cold seasons if fruits do not seem to be setting and starting to swell, it may be necessary to help fertilization by hand pollinating. Pick off a male flower, and after removing the petals, push it firmly into the centre of a female flower.

Marrows and gourds often throw out roots from the stems. These can be earthed over to encourage rooting and so increase the plant's food and water supply. Liquid feeding during growth is beneficial, particularly as fruits are swelling.

Harvesting

Courgettes should be cut regularly when about 4 inches long (10 cm), from July to September. Where grown primarily for large marrows, start picking when fruits are 6 to 8 inches long (15–20 cm) to encourage further fruiting. A few can be left to develop to full size for storage.

Where pumpkins are being grown limit production to 2 or 3 fruits per plant, removing the tips of shoots and surplus fruits towards the end of summer. Gourds for storage can be left on the plants as long as possible to ripen and harden, cutting away any foliage that shades them. Cut them off the plants before frost, with as long a piece of stem as possible. Dry off for a few more days in the sun if necessary and store them on racks in a well-ventilated, frost-free shed, or suspended in nets. Ordinary marrows can normally be stored until around Christmas; most winter gourds until early spring the following year. See also p. 42.

Pests and diseases

Marrows are relatively disease free when grown outdoors, provided they are in a well-drained position. Protect young seedlings against slugs (see p. iv). Cucumber mosaic virus can be serious in some seasons (see pp. ii, viii). Withering of the fruit, starting at the blossom end, sometimes occurs, due to faulty root action. Check that the plant has not been affected by foot or root rot, and if so, destroy

Courgettes, which are immature marrows, ready for picking.

Typical mature marrow which can be used fresh or stored for short periods.

it. If not, rest the plant by removing the fruit, water carefully, and if the leaves are a poor colour spray with a foliar feed. The plant should regain its vigour and start to fruit normally.

Some recommended cultivars

F_1 bush hybrids suitable for courgettes: Early Gem, Emerald Cross, Greyzini, Golden Zucchini.
Bush: All Green Bush, Long Green Bush, Long White Bush, Table Dainty (semi-bush).
Trailing: Trailing Long Green, Trailing Long White.

PUMPKINS

Keeping a pumpkin within bounds. The plant is trained into a circle.

A mature pumpkin set against a wall to ripen and allow the skin to harden.

Onions & related species

Many types of onions are grown. Spring onions are grown for the white shank, and various types of evergreen onions for the fresh green leaf; others are grown for the bulb, either used immature or stored for use in winter. Very small onions are grown primarily for pickling. Most of the onions grown in this country are yellow or brown skinned with white flesh, but there are others with red skin and flesh.

Site/soil

Onions require an open site and a fertile, well-drained soil. Acid soils will need liming. The soil should be thoroughly dug several months in advance – in the case of spring-sown onions in the autumn before sowing – working in well-rotted manure or compost. Onions should not be sown on freshly manured ground. They should be rotated on at least a 3-year cycle to avoid the build-up of certain soil-borne diseases and pests.

Bulb onions

These can be raised either from seed or sets, which are specially produced bulblets. For large bulbs or storage onions, as long a growing season as possible is needed, so that the bulbs have time to develop, mature and dry before storing. An all-year-round supply of bulb onions can be ensured by making two sowings or plantings. The first is in spring, for onions harvested from August to October. The second is to sow the Japanese over-wintering cultivars to give supplies in June and July of the following year. (An onion set for autumn planting has also been recently introduced.)

Raising from seed. Prepare a fairly firmly consolidated seedbed with a fine tilth. Onion seed germinates slowly in cold wet soils and is susceptible to damping off and other diseases, so where possible warm the soil with cloches before sowing. Sow outdoors as soon as soil conditions are reasonable, from February to early April. Sow very thinly in drills $\frac{1}{2}$ to $\frac{3}{4}$ inch deep (2 cm), in rows 12 inches apart (30 cm). If available use seed treated against fungus infection.

Once the onions have germinated, thin (if necessary) until they are $1\frac{1}{2}$ inches apart (4 cm); this spacing will give the maximum yield of medium sized onions. Space at 3 or 4 inches apart (8–10 cm) if extra large onions are required. Larger thinnings can be used as salad onions.

ONIONS

Thinning spring onions in a sown row: the thinnings are used in salads.

Planting onion sets: the bulblets are planted below the surface (see left-hand row) to protect them from birds.

Onions being dried off after harvesting on a raised support of wire netting.

Mature onion suitable for storage (left); and an unsuitable, bull-necked bulb (right).

To extend the growing season onions can be started off earlier by sowing in gentle heat indoors in January or early February. Prick out into seed trays or individual pots, or sow direct into soil blocks. Harden off well before planting out in March. Transplanted seedlings may need to be watered carefully in the early stages of growth.

Germination of onion seed can also be accelerated by fluid sowing (see p. 25). Both the use of fluid sowing and the use of transplants raised indoors lead to higher yields.

Raising onions from sets. Sets have several advantages over seed. They are easier to grow, less prone to disease, can give reasonable crops in poor soil conditions, and because they are already of some substance, they mature earlier than seed-raised onions. They are often used where onion fly is a serious problem. Their disadvantages are that they are more expensive, that only certain cultivars are available, and that they are more likely to bolt (i.e. run to seed) resulting in poor onions which cannot be stored. Bolting is minimized by selecting small rather than large sets and, if available, using heat-treated sets.

Plant the sets as soon as soil conditions allow from February to early April. Heat-treated sets should not be planted until late March or early April. Plant in rows 10 inches apart (25 cm), putting them in gently without firming, so that only the tips protrude above soil level. If planted more shallowly birds are liable to uproot them. For maximum yields of good-sized bulbs they should be planted at 2 inches apart (5 cm) in the rows. Larger individual bulbs will be obtained if they are spaced at 3 or 4 inches apart (8–10 cm).

Cultivation

Onions are particularly susceptible to weed competition in the first 6 weeks after sowing or planting. So it is important to keep the area well weeded in the early stages, both in the rows and between the plants. For fertilizers and rates of application see p. 11. Watering is generally unnecessary after the plants have become established except in very dry weather. If bulb onions are watered later than mid-July maturity may be delayed and keeping quality impaired.

Harvesting and storage

Bulbs can be pulled for use fresh at any stage. They are ready to harvest for storage when the foliage starts to die back and the tops to bend over. There is no need to bend over the tops by hand. Do not keep thick-stemmed onions as they do not store well. Stored onions rarely keep well beyond April. (For storage, see pp. 42, 43.)

Autumn-sown crop

The hardy Japanese cultivars mature in June and July in the year after sowing, filling the gap between stored onions and the spring-sown crop. The date of sowing is critical for success and this varies with location:

the first week of August in the north of England and Scotland;

the second and third weeks in August for the Midlands, the south and south-east of England;

the last week in August for the south-west including south Wales.

If sown too early they become too large and may bolt in spring; if sown too late they will be very small, and may not survive the winter. The onions should be about 6 to 8 inches tall (15–20 cm) in October.

Choose a plot that is well drained, and incorporate Growmore at 4 to 6 oz/sq. yd (130–200 g/m^2) before sowing. These bulb onions have a relatively high requirement of nitrogen.

Sow the seed an inch apart (2.5 cm) in drills 12 inches apart (30 cm). In very hot weather the seed may not germinate well; watering several times after sowing, or covering the seedbed with white reflective material, helps to lower the temperature and encourage germination.

A top-dressing of Nitrochalk at the rate of 2 to 3 oz per sq. yd (70–100 g/m^2) is recommended for early January to get a good crop and reduce rotting. In spring the onions can be thinned to 2 inches apart (5 cm). The Japanese onions can be harvested from early June up to August, but cannot be stored for the winter.

Several older cultivars of onions were traditionally sown in August in mild parts of the country, thinning to about an inch apart (2.5 cm) in autumn, and thinning or transplanting in spring. These varieties are less hardy and reliable in winter and later maturing than the newer ones.

Pickling onions

These will tolerate poorer and drier soils than bulb or spring onions, but do better on fertile soil. Sow

PICKLING ONIONS

Pickling onions grown in a wide drill; seeds sown $\frac{1}{4}$ inch apart and not thinned.

Paris Silverskin pickling onions being dried off before use.

seeds in March or April. For pickling onions a population of 30 plants per sq. foot is best. So when sowing in rows 12 inches apart (30 cm), sow at about $\frac{1}{4}$ inch apart (6 mm); allowing for non-germination this should give the right plant numbers. Pickling onions can also be sown in bands about 9 inches wide (22 cm). There is no need to thin them out, as competition keeps the bulbs small. They are normally ready in August. After the foliage has died down they can be lifted as bulb onions, and stored until required for pickling.

Bunching or spring onions

These are grown primarily for use of the small white shank and green leaves in salads. The thinnings from maincrop onions can be used in the same way.

The soil and seedbed is prepared as for bulb onions. Sow from March to June at intervals of 2 to 3 weeks for continuous supplies in summer and autumn. Sow the extra hardy cultivars (such as White Lisbon) in July (in the north), and August (in the south), for an overwintering crop which will be ready for use the following March to May.

The highest yields are obtained by sowing in rows 4 inches apart (10 cm), aiming for 30 plants per sq. foot. Alternatively spring onions can be grown in bands 3 inches wide (8 cm), with 6 inches (15 cm) between the bands. Sow thinly so that there is no need to thin further; the onions can be pulled as required.

They can be watered at any stage if the soil gets dry, at the rate of 1 gal./20 foot row (1 litre/1.3 m of row). The winter crop can be given cloche protection in cold areas.

Pests and diseases

The most common pest is onion fly, which is especially serious on dry soils (see p. vi). Stem and bulb eelworm can also be serious on infected soils (see p. vi).

The most common diseases are downy mildew, white rot, and neck rot in stored onions. Losses from *Botrytis* in overwintered crops can be serious.

Some recommended cultivars

Bulb onions suitable for storage: (spring sown) Hydura F_1, Hygro F_1, Rijnsburger-Balstora, Rijnsburger-Robusta; (autumn sowing and spring

transplanting) Reliance (Autumn Queen); (from sets) Sturon, Stuttgart Giant (Stuttgarter Riesen).
Japanese autumn-sown onions:
Express Yellow F_1, Imai Early Yellow, Senshyu Semi-globe Yellow.
Autumn planted set: Unwins First Early.
Spring onions:
Spring sown: White Lisbon.
August sown: Winter Hardy, White Lisbon.
Pickling onion:
Barletta, Paris Silver Skin.

PERENNIAL GREEN ONIONS

Welsh onion (Ciboule)

This is a relatively hardy, perennial, evergreen onion, growing to about 2 feet tall (60 cm) in clumps. The hollow leaves remain green all year, making it a useful supply of green leaf. The base of the stem is thickened but does not form a true bulb.

Welsh onions can be sown in spring in rows 9 inches apart (22 cm), thinning to 8 inches apart (20 cm). These will be ready during the summer. They can also be sown in August for use in the following spring. Single leaves can be cut, or an individual plant or the whole clump lifted for use.

The clumps become thicker every year, and to keep them growing vigorously lift them every 2 to 3 years in spring or autumn, dividing and replanting the young parts at about 8 inches apart (20 cm).

Where the climate is severe Welsh onions are treated as annuals or biennials and sown annually, as seed-raised plants are said to be hardier than those raised by division.

The Everlasting or Ever-ready onion

This is similar to the Welsh onion, though dwarfer in habit, with finer, flatter leaves. It also remains green throughout winter. It is grown and used like Welsh onion, though it has to be propagated by division as the plant does not produce seeds.

Chives

One of the most commonly grown herbs, chives are a good substitute for spring onions, though they have a distinct flavour of their own. Sow chives in spring, planting out 2 to 3 seedlings together in clumps 9 inches apart (22 cm). Once established the clumps can be divided every few years in spring or autumn, and small clumps of a few plants be replanted.

Chives should be cut back to ground level several times during the season to encourage the vigorous growth of leaves. Unless grown for their decorative value, the flowering heads should also be cut back. The foliage dies down in winter, but if a few plants are cloched they will start growing early in the year.

CHIVES

Dividing up a mature plant for replanting, leaving several small plants in each cluster.

Shallots

Shallots are large bulbs with a very distinct flavour, used raw, cooked and pickled. They are very easy to grow and excellent for storage, keeping firm longer than any other onion. There are red and yellow forms.

Site/soil

(See onions)

Cultivation

Shallots are usually raised from sets, each shallot set multiplying into a clump. Buy stocks that are certified as virus-free wherever possible. Small sets are preferable to large, as they are less likely to bolt, and will produce a clump of reasonably sized shallots. Larger sets tend to produce a larger clump of smaller shallots. The ideal size is about $\frac{1}{3}$ oz (10 g) in weight, about $\frac{3}{4}$ inch in diameter (2 cm).

Shallots need as long a growing season as possible. On well-drained soil in mild areas they can be planted in December and January; otherwise plant in February and March, as soon as the soil can be worked. Remove loose scales and plant in a drill so that only the tips protrude. If they are planted shallowly they are likely to be uprooted by birds. Any that are uprooted should be lifted completely and replanted, not just pushed back into the soil, which breaks the roots. To get maximum yields of good-sized shallots plant small sets 6 inches apart (15 cm) in rows 8 inches apart (20 cm), and large sets 6 inches apart (15 cm) in rows 12 inches apart (30 cm). Small sets can be planted at 1 inch square (2.5 cm) to give early crops of salad onions. If planted in seed boxes in a greenhouse they can be harvested very early.

If necessary water after planting, giving up to $\frac{1}{8}$ pint (70 ml) per day per plant. They rarely require watering after they are established. Keep the crop weeded during growth.

Harvesting

During the summer a few shoots can be used as green onions if required. Bulbs are ready for harvesting in July and August. Lift the bulbs, allowing them to dry for a few days, and store on trays or in net bags in a frost-free place (see p. 42). If stored well they will keep satisfactorily until June the following year. Reserve a few healthy bulbs of about $\frac{3}{4}$ inch diameter (2 cm) for planting the following year.

Pests and diseases

Shallots are normally a trouble-free crop. The most likely pests are onion fly and stem and bulb eelworm (see p. vi).

Garlic

The strong flavoured cloves of garlic are widely used in cooking. Garlic is very hardy, and far more easily grown in this country than is generally realized. There are pink and white forms.

Site/soil

Garlic requires an open sunny position and preferably light, well-drained soil for the best results. Where grown on heavy soil a little sand or ashes worked into the bottom of the drill will help to improve drainage. The soil should have been manured for the previous crop.

SHALLOTS

Planting shallots with the old stem just above the surface.

A good row of shallots, well weeded.

Cultivation
Garlic is normally raised by planting the individual cloves, which are split off from the large bulb. It needs as long a growing season as possible. The main planting period is September to November, which will provide fresh garlic early the following summer, and allow time for the crop to mature, be lifted and dried for winter storage. Alternatively plant from February to March, as early as soil conditions allow, although a crop from this planting may not ripen well in poor summers.

Plant firm individual cloves about 4 inches apart (10 cm) in drills about 1½ inches deep (4 cm), so that only the tip protrudes above soil level. On very heavy soils garlic is sometimes planted on ridges for better drainage. Rows can be 6 inches apart (15 cm). Keep the crop weed free during growth.

Harvesting
Harvest as for storage onions (see p. 106), drying them in the sun as long as possible outside, and finishing them by hanging them in bunches in a sunny greenhouse or conservatory until the bulbs are blanched white. Store in a dry, frost-free place (see p. 42). If dried and stored well garlic can keep for up to 10 months, but it will rot in damp conditions.

GARLIC

The separated cloves being planted in a shallow drill.

A loose bunch of garlic hung up for winter storage.

Parsley

Parsley is a biennial herb, running to seed in its second year. It is the most commonly used herb in English cooking, and besides its decorative and seasoning qualities, it is very rich in vitamins. Both the leaves and the stems can be used. Parsley is difficult to dry satisfactorily, but can be frozen well.

Parsley is relatively hardy, but the quality of the foliage deteriorates in winter. Unless protected, the plants tend to die back or die off completely in severe weather.

There are two main forms, the curled and the French, plain or broad-leaved. The curled is more popular, but the broad-leaved is said to be better flavoured and is easier to grow.

Hamburg or turnip-rooted parsley is a dual-purpose form: the smooth parsnip-like roots make an excellent winter vegetable, while the plain leaves remain green throughout winter, withstanding more severe weather than ordinary parsley and forming a useful substitute. It is grown and used as parsnips.

Site/soil

Parsley can be grown in sunny or partially shaded positions. It requires reasonably fertile, moisture-retentive soil, and does not generally do well on poor or very light soils.

Cultivation

To ensure continuous supplies of good-quality parsley it is advisable to make two sowings a year. Sow in March for the main summer supply, and again in June or July, to give a fresh crop for autumn and early winter.

Parsley is normally sown direct, in drills ½ to ¾ inch deep (2 cm), aiming for plants at 6 inches apart (10 cm). Germination is often very slow, taking as long as four to six weeks. Avoid sowing in cold wet soils. Germination can be accelerated by watering the drills with boiling water before sowing, or lining the drills with moist peat. It is important to keep the soil moist until the seed has germinated. Parsley is a suitable crop for fluid sowing (see pp. 24–5), which gives considerably earlier and better emergence. It can also be sown indoors in soil blocks and the young seedlings transplanted.

During the growing season the plants need to be kept weed free, and well watered when dry.

Parsley is cut as required. The plants can be cut back to ground level once or twice during the year. At the onset of cold weather parsley can be protected with bracken or cloches, which prolongs the supply of good-quality parsley. Such protected plants often provide the first fresh green parsley in the following spring.

Alternatively, in September a few plants from the second sowing can be potted up and brought indoors, or planted in a cold greenhouse, for a protected winter supply.

Pests and diseases

The most likely problems are carrot fly (see pp. i, v) and aphids. Severely stunted growth is sometimes caused by the carrot motley dwarf virus, which is aphid transmitted. Burn any infected plants.

Cultivars

Some recommended cultivars of curled parsley: Bravour, Moss Curled, Paramount.

HAMBURG PARSLEY

This unusual type of parsley is grown for root and leaf, both for winter use.

TYPES OF PARSLEY

Broad-leaved type.

Curled type.

Parsnip

Parsnips are a very valuable winter root vegetable. There are long and short rooted types, the latter being recommended for shallow soils.

Site/soil

Parsnips require an open site. They grow best on light, deep, well-cultivated soil, preferably stone-free, but will grow satisfactorily on most soils. They should not, however, be planted on freshly manured ground or roots are likely to be forked. Work the seedbed into a fine tilth before sowing, incorporating a general fertilizer (see p. 11).

Cultivation

Always use fresh seed, as it rapidly loses its viability. It also germinates slowly and erratically in cold conditions, and sowings in April or May are more successful than those earlier in February or March. The risk of canker infection is also reduced by later sowing. Parsnips can also be started indoors in gentle heat, preferably in soil blocks. Fluid sowing will give considerably faster germination (see p. 25).

The best method of sowing parsnips outdoors is to sow 2 or 3 seeds at each site at $\frac{1}{2}$ to $\frac{3}{4}$ inch deep (2 cm). If large roots are required (crowns over 2 inch diameter (5 cm or more)) grow large rooted cultivars such as Offenham in rows 12 inches apart (30 cm), at 6 inches apart in the rows (15 cm). For smaller roots (crowns $1\frac{1}{2}$ to 2 inches diameter: 4–5 cm), sow at 3 inches apart (8 cm) in rows 8 inches apart (20 cm). Thin to one plant after germination.

PARSNIP

Sowing three seeds at each position in the drill. After germination one seedling is left.

Parsnips can be intersown with radishes or small lettuces. These mark the rows until the parsnips germinate, so making weeding easier.

Watering is generally only necessary in very dry weather, when steady growth can be maintained by watering every two to three weeks, at the rate of about 2 gal./sq. yd (11 litres/m^2). This will improve the quality and size of the roots. Roots are likely to split if water is suddenly supplied (naturally or artificially) after a prolonged dry spell.

Harvesting

Roots are normally ready from October onwards. They are very hardy and can be left in the soil all winter, lifting as required. However, as the foliage dies down completely, their position in the soil should be marked. A layer of straw or bracken will help to make lifting easier in frosty weather. Any remaining roots can be lifted in March and heeled in, or stored in sand, to prevent re-sprouting.

Pests and diseases

The most common pests are celery fly (see p. vi) and carrot fly (pp. i, v); the most serious disease, particularly in old garden soils, is canker (see p. viii).

Some recommended cultivars

Short rooted: Avonresister (highly resistant to canker), Offenham (susceptible to canker), White Gem (resistant to canker).
Long rooted: Lisbonnais, Tender and True.

TYPES OF PARSNIP

Parsnip roots ready for use: they can be kept in the ground until ready for use.

Peas

Ordinary garden peas are grown for the peas inside the pod. They are either wrinkle or round seeded, the former being the sweeter, but the latter hardier and therefore used for very late and very early sowings. Petit Pois are a distinct form of very small garden pea, which have an excellent flavour.

Garden peas vary in height from 1½ feet tall (45 cm) to 5 feet (1.5 m). They are grouped by season into earlies, second earlies (or early maincrop), and maincrop. Depending on day temperature earlies mature on average in 11 to 12 weeks, second earlies in 12 to 13 weeks and maincrop in 13 to 14 weeks, progressing from shorter, lower yielding cultivars which require less space, to taller, higher yielding ones which require considerable space. Earlies and early maincrop cultivars are more suited to small gardens and light soils, and can be sown in succession throughout the summer.

Sugar or mangetout peas are a different type in which the entire pod is eaten when the peas are immature. Some of the new cultivars are dual purpose; the pods can be eaten whole when young, or shelled for the peas at a later stage. Mangetout peas appear to be easier to grow than garden peas, and have an excellent flavour. They range from dwarf to about 5 feet high (1.5 m).

Both garden and mangetout peas can be frozen. Garden peas can also be shelled and dried for winter use.

Site/soil

Peas require an open but not exposed position. They are by nature a cool weather crop, growing best in spring and cool summers, and disliking intense heat, drought, and poorly drained soils. Provided it has ample moisture, the summer crop can be grown in light shade. The soil needs to be fertile and deeply cultivated, preferably working in manure or compost the autumn before sowing to make the soil as moisture retentive as possible. A trench can be dug as for beans incorporating manure or compost into the lower spit (see p. 65). Peas should be rotated to avoid any build-up of soil-borne diseases.

Cultivation

Peas germinate poorly in cold soils, and where germination is slow, losses are liable to be high due to mice damage, and fungus and bacterial diseases attacking the seeds. Little is gained by sowing early in a cold spring.

In warm areas the earliest outdoor sowings,

SOWING PEAS

A flat-bottomed drill with three rows of peas sown about 2 inches apart.

A single row sown in a V-shaped drill.

which will be ready at the end of May or early June, can be made in a sheltered position from late February onwards. Where possible, sow under cloches. Alternatively warm the soil in advance with cloches, or take out the drill on a sunny morning, and leave it for a few hours before sowing. It is advisable to use seed treated against fungus diseases for early sowings.

For the main summer crop, maturing from mid-June onwards, sow seeds of early or second early cultivars at intervals of about 3 to 4 weeks from April to early July, or sow cultivars from different seasonal groups on the same date in April or May, to give staggered maturity.

In July sow an early dwarf cultivar, which will crop in autumn if the weather remains fine.

In mild parts of the country hardy overwintering early peas can be sown outdoors in October or November for an early crop in the following year. The success of this crop depends on the winter weather, so cloche protection is advisable.

Sow seeds 1 to $1\frac{1}{2}$ inches deep (4 cm). There are various patterns of sowing. Traditionally peas are sown about 2 inches apart (5 cm), either in a 9 inch wide (22 cm), flat bottomed drill, or in a single row in a V-shaped drill. The distance between the drills or single rows is about the height of the peas at maturity. A modern recommendation is to sow in bands of 3 rows, each row $4\frac{1}{2}$ inches apart (12 cm), with the seeds $4\frac{1}{2}$ inches apart (12 cm) within the rows, and 18 inches between the bands (45 cm). Peas are also grown successfully in plots 3 to 4 feet wide (1 m), the peas at equidistant spacing 2 to 3 inches apart (5–7 cm).

Whatever method is used, yields are increased if peas are given support from an early stage, as soon as the tendrils appear, using pea sticks, wide mesh wire netting or nylon net. The support for a single row can be on one side of the row; for wide drills or bands it can run down the centre or be on either side; where grown in a patch wire netting can be staked around the edge of the patch, as the peas in the centre more or less support each other.

The commonest causes of failure with peas are mice eating the seed, and birds attacking both the seedlings and the pods. When making the early and overwintered sowings it is advisable to set mouse traps alongside the rows, putting them under tiles to keep the bait dry and the birds away.

All sowings need to be protected from birds in the early stages (until supports are erected), with

PEA SEEDLINGS

Netting guard for protection against birds (close the ends). Strands of black cotton are also effective.

Peas at the stage when they need to be supported: the tendrils are now visible.

METHODS OF SUPPORT

The traditional pea sticks set on either side of a wide drill.

Nylon netting supported on a triangular framework.

TYPES OF PEAS

Left, garden pea, and right petit pois.

Above, mangetout or sugar peas.

black cotton strung over the rows, or by using wire or net pea guards.

Young plants need to be hoed carefully or hand weeded. The stems of the overwintered and early spring sowings can be earthed up a little to give them extra support.

Unless conditions are very dry in the early stages of growth, watering is unnecessary until the peas start to flower. Watering at the rate of 4 gal./sq. yd (22 litres/m^2)/week, from the start of flowering and throughout the pod forming and picking period will increase both the yields and quality of the crop.

Peas benefit from being mulched, to conserve the moisture in the soil and keep the roots cool.

Harvesting

Pick peas regularly to encourage further cropping, and to have them in their prime. Sugar peas can be picked when the tiny pea is just visible as a swelling inside the pod.

Where peas are to be dried leave them on the plant as long as possible, and then hang the bundles of uprooted vines in an airy sheltered place until the pods are dry enough to split open.

Pests and diseases

Apart from birds and mice, the most serious pest is pea moth (see p. v). In hot seasons, pea thrips can be damaging (see p. v). Seedlings damp off and are prone to various rots if sown in cold wet conditions.

Some recommended cultivars (wrinkled seeded)

Early: Hurst Beagle (suitable for overwintering).
Second early/early maincrop: Early Onward, Hurst Canice, Kelvedon Wonder, Victory Freezer.
Maincrop: Hurst Greenshaft, Lincoln.
Sugar peas (mangetout): Sugar Snap, Tezieravenir.

SUPPORT WITH NETTING

Sheep netting is another firm support for peas.

Potatoes

Potato cultivars are grouped according to the season of lifting as earlies, second earlies and maincrop. Early potatoes mature in 100 to 110 days, second earlies in 110 to 120 days, and maincrop in 125 to 140 days depending on the weather. Generally speaking the early groups are lower yielding, require less space, escape some of the diseases which affect the maincrop potatoes, and are ready for use in June or early July when potato prices in shops are still high.

Maincrop potatoes are normally ready from late July onwards, and are either lifted for immediate use or, when fully mature, stored for winter supplies. As they take up considerable space for much of the growing season, in a small garden it is probably only worth growing early potatoes, where the difference in quality between home-grown and shop-bought is most marked.

Site/soil

Potatoes require an open site; frost pockets should be avoided for early potatoes, as there is a danger that the young shoots may be damaged by a late frost. Acid soils (pH 5 to 6) are preferred, but potatoes will grow on a wide range of soils, doing best on deep, fertile, well-drained but moisture-retentive soil. They should always be grown on a three-year rotation to avoid the build-up of eelworm.

Prepare the soil by digging in plenty of farmyard manure or compost in the autumn before planting. Maincrop potatoes have very high nitrogen requirements (see p. 11), the early crop slightly lower nitrogen requirements. Potatoes are often the first crop to be planted in new gardens on 'new' soils; although their yields may not be high, they help to improve the soil structure with their extensive root system.

Cultivation

Potatoes are raised by planting seed potatoes. These are small potatoes, grown in areas where the risk of virus infection is lowest. Wherever possible buy best-quality, certified seed potatoes.

Provided the soil is fertile and disease free, the key to a high yield of potatoes is plenty of moisture throughout growth, and a long growing season. As potatoes are susceptible to frost, the growing season is extended by starting potatoes into growth indoors, a process known as 'sprouting' or 'chitting'. This is most valuable for early cultivars.

Chitting. The normal method is to buy certified seed potatoes in February, and to place the tubers in shallow trays, in the light but not in direct sunlight, in a frost-free shed or cool room. Stand them upright side by side, with the 'rose' end uppermost; this is the end in which most of the dormant sprouts (potato eyes) are concentrated. Chitting takes about six weeks, during which time several shoots develop. The potatoes are ready for planting when the shoots are $\frac{3}{4}$ to 1 inch long (2.5 cm); if the shoots are longer, they will need to be handled very carefully so that they are not broken in planting.

If large-sized, early potatoes are wanted surplus sprouts can be rubbed off at planting, leaving only 2 or 3 on a plant; this will not result in as high a yield. With maincrop potatoes the aim is to have as many eyes and sprouts as possible.

Planting. Planting can begin in mid-March, starting with the earliest cultivars. The potatoes can be planted a couple of weeks earlier, either by planting under cloches or by covering the potatoes after planting with perforated transparent plastic film which will help to keep off frost. This film is 'expandable' and is pushed up by the growing plants. It can be removed three to four weeks after the first potato leaves have appeared. The young growths of early potatoes can also be protected from late frost by drawing up a little soil over them, or by covering them with several inches of bracken or straw. Planting can continue in April and May. Close planting of small tubers in June and July will give 'new potatoes' late in the year.

A general fertilizer can be worked into the soil just before planting, followed by a top-dressing of nitrogen during growth (see p. 11).

The highest yields of large potatoes are obtained by planting fairly small seed potatoes, about the size of a hen's egg. The old practice of cutting large potatoes in half is not recommended as it encourages disease. Reject any diseased potatoes.

A drill 4 to 5 inches deep (10–12 cm) is made with a draw hoe or spade, or individual holes made with a trowel. Plant the rose end uppermost, so that the seed is covered by about an inch of soil (2.5 cm). If the tubers have been sprouted, take care not to break the sprouts in planting and when raking the soil back into the drill or hole.

Early potatoes are planted at 15 inches apart (38 cm) in rows 15 to 18 inches apart (38–45 cm). Maincrop potatoes are normally grown at 15 inches

POTATOES

Well-sprouted tubers ready for planting out.

Planting the sprouted tubers in a drill.

Earthing up: this will need to be done two or three times during the growing season.

Cutting the potato haulm in late August, to prevent the spread of blight.

Filling in the drill carefully, to leave a slight mound over the row, which helps to protect the young shoots from an early frost.

After lifting, the potatoes are left to dry for a few hours before storing.

apart (38 cm), in rows 30 inches apart (76 cm). However, optimum yields are obtained by varying the spacing according to the size of the tuber and the growth characteristics of the variety.

Potatoes are earthed up during growth, to prevent the greening of tubers which are pushed to the surface. Green potatoes are poisonous and should never be eaten. Earthing up is best done in one operation when the plants are about 9 inches high (22 cm), drawing earth to 4 to 5 inches high (10–12 cm) around the stems of the plant.

Several methods can be adopted to avoid earthing up. One is to plant very small tubers, each about $\frac{1}{3}$ oz (10 g) in weight, about 4 inches deep (10 cm), about 10 inches apart (25 cm). With this moderately close spacing of small tubers none are forced to the surface and the crop can be grown flat. It will give reasonable yields.

The potato row can also be covered with black plastic sheeting after planting (see p. 120). The sheeting is anchored at the edges into the soil. When the leaves push up the plastic, slits are cut in it and the young growths pulled through. When ready the potatoes are easily lifted from the surface after pulling back the plastic. Weed growth is also prevented.

The yield, quality and earliness of potatoes is influenced by the water supply. With early potatoes, *highest yields* are obtained by watering every 10 to 14 days in dry weather during the growing period, at the rate of 3 to 4 gal./sq. yd (16–22 litres/m^2). The potatoes should not be lifted until the foliage starts to die back. However, if *very early* potatoes are wanted, the plants should be watered when the tubers are just starting to form and are the size of marbles. This usually coincides with flowering. Water at similar rates as above.

With maincrop potatoes, watering is generally unnecessary until the marble stage. A single heavy watering of about 4 to 5 gal./sq. yd (22–27 litres/m^2) at this stage increases both the total yield and tuber size. Watering can start about 10 days earlier with small tubered varieties. There is some evidence that watering reduces the number of potatoes with common scab.

If the crop has been affected by potato blight (see p. viii) the haulm should be cut back to a couple of inches above ground level in late August to prevent the spread of blight. Otherwise, if the plants are healthy and growing conditions good, they will continue to bulk up in September, and the

PLANTING UNDER PLASTIC

Planting potatoes under black plastic; no earthing up is needed.

At the end of the season when the plastic is pulled away the potatoes are ready to lift.

haulm can be cut back some time during that month. Cutting the haulm also makes the crop easier to lift.

Harvesting

Early potatoes and maincrop potatoes for immediate use are lifted as required. Remove even very small potatoes, which if left can carry over disease. Potatoes required for storage should be left in the ground a couple of weeks after the haulm has been cut so that the skins will harden. Choose a good drying day, and lift them carefully to minimize damage, leaving them on the surface to dry for two to three hours before being stored (see p. 40). Reject any diseased or damaged tubers. Potatoes should keep in reasonable condition until May or June the following year. They should always be kept in the dark, or they turn green.

Pests and diseases

The most serious pests are wireworm, cutworm, slugs and various species of potato cyst eelworm (see pp. iii, vi). Potato blight, common scab, potato mosaic virus and potato leaf roll virus are the most serious diseases (see p. viii).

Some recommended cultivars

Earlies: Duke of York, Epicure, Foremost, Maris Bard, Pentland Javelin, Ulster Sceptre; *with some eelworm resistance:* Maris Anchor, Pentland Javelin, Pentland Lustre.

Maincrop: Desiree, King Edward, Maris Piper, Pentland Dell, Record; *with some eelworm resistance:* Cara, Klondyke, Maris Piper, Paragon; *with slug resistance:* Stormont Enterprise.

Radish

Radishes can be available from the garden all year round. The familiar summer radishes are small, round or long in shape, with skins red, white, or mixed red and white. They have to be used when mature or they become woody, hollow and run to seed. Winter radishes are enormous in comparison, some reaching several pounds in weight. They do not deteriorate when mature, but can be stored or lifted for winter use. They vary considerably in colour and shape. Radish pods are also edible.

RADISHES

Radishes are a useful crop for intersowing, here between parsnips.

Types of winter radishes, left to right, Black Spanish Long, Japanese type, Black Spanish Round, China Rose.

Soil/situation

Radishes normally require an open site, though mid-summer sowings can be made in light shade, or intersown between other crops. Soil should be light, rich and well drained, manured for a previous crop. Rich sandy soils are ideal.

The best-quality radishes in the summer are obtained when the crop is grown quickly with adequate moisture during growth.

Radishes need to be rotated as for brassicas, as they are subject to the same diseases. This is more important for winter radishes, which are in the soil for a long period, than for the summer radishes, which may be ready within a month from sowing.

Radishes are very useful for intersowing (see p. 26). The seed can also be mixed with the seed of a slow germinating crop such as parsnip or parsley, and used to mark the rows. The radishes germinate first, and will be pulled for use long before they disturb the growth of the main crop in the row.

Cultivation

Radish seed retains its viability (in proper storage) for up to 10 years, and germinates in a wide range of soil temperatures.

Summer radishes can be sown outdoors from February (in warm situations and light soil) until September. The season can be extended at both ends by sowing in cold frames or under cloches from September to November, and again from February to April. Cultivars which make less top growth are more suited for these protected sowings (see below).

Sow the seed $\frac{1}{2}$ to $\frac{3}{4}$ inch deep (2 cm), as thinly as possible, spacing seeds about an inch apart (2.5 cm). Radishes never develop well if at any stage the seedlings are overcrowded and become leggy. The rows can be about 6 inches apart (15 cm).

Radishes mature rapidly so it is best to make small regular sowings at weekly or fortnightly intervals throughout the summer. Except in very wet weather, water the bottom of the drill before sowing, covering the seeds with dry soil to prevent evaporation. This encourages quick germination. For fertilizer requirements see p. 11.

Radishes will grow rapidly in warm weather and moist soil, but too much water will result in excess leafage. In dry weather 2 gal. per sq. yd. (11 litres/m^2) per week should be enough for balanced growth. As mentioned above seeds need moist soil for quick germination.

Winter radishes are sown in July and early August in rows 8 to 10 inches apart (20–25 cm). Again, it is most important to sow thinly, but, if necessary, thin the seedlings to 4 to 6 inches apart (10–15 cm). At this usually dry time watering the drill before sowing will also help germination. In dry weather, after germination, water weekly at the rate of approximately 2 gal./sq. yd (22 litres/m^2). Too much water encourages the growth of leaf at the expense of the root.

Harvesting

Summer radishes are pulled as required. Winter radishes can be left in the ground during the winter, and covered with straw to make lifting easier in frosty weather. Alternatively they can be lifted in the autumn, the tops trimmed, and stored in boxes (see p. 40). This may be advisable in heavy soils where slug damage is serious.

Radish pods can be picked when they are green and break in half crisply. If no radishes have run to seed naturally, a few radishes left in the ground will eventually do so.

Pests

The most serious pest is flea beetle (see p. v) which attacks seedlings. Slugs may also be a problem, nibbling the roots in the ground, especially of winter radishes (see p. iv).

Some recommended cultivars

Summer radish: ★Cherry Belle, ★French Breakfast, Red Prince (Prinz Rotin), ★Robino, ★Rota, ★Saxa, Sparkler.
Winter radish: Black Spanish Long, Black Spanish Round, China Rose.
★ also suited for sowing under glass for early and late crops

Rhubarb

Rhubarb is a hardy perennial plant, grown for its long leaf stalks which are used blanched or in their natural state. It provides a valuable crop early in the year.

Site/soil

Rhubarb is deep rooting, and will grow on almost any soil type, including peat, sand or clay, provided it is well drained and fertile. It will tolerate an acid soil. However, it needs an open site and should not be grown in the shade.

Cultivation

In good conditions plants can spread to 6 feet across (1.8 m), so plenty of space should be allowed. Prepare the soil beforehand by digging deeply, working in plenty of farmyard manure or compost, and removing perennial weeds. Where soil is very heavy or waterlogged, rhubarb can be planted on ridges.

Rhubarb is grown from divisions of old plants, each of which needs at least one bud and a piece of the root stock. They can either be bought, or an old plant dug up and divided. Two- or 3-year-old crowns can be divided with a spade into 3 to 6 divisions. If older crowns are divided take the buds from the outside as the centre ones tend to be less vigorous. When starting obtain a good named cultivar or take a division from a vigorous healthy plant.

November is probably the best time to plant rhubarb, but it can be planted any time between October and March, when the plant is dormant. Plant the divisions at 2½ to 3 feet apart (60–75 cm). With cultivars with large buds and producing thick stems, e.g. The Sutton, plant with the bud just above the soil surface, otherwise they may rot. Other cultivars with smaller buds, e.g. Timperley Early can be planted with an inch or two of soil (2.5–5 cm) above the buds.

Rhubarb can also be raised from seed, although there will be considerable variation in the quality of the plants. Seed is sown in March or April in a seedbed, in drills about an inch deep (2.5 cm), thinning to 6 inches apart (15 cm). The young plants are planted out in their permanent positions in the autumn or following spring. Start pulling in the second season after planting.

Rhubarb needs plenty of moisture and will respond to watering in most seasons. Plants benefit from being kept well mulched. After the leaves die

RHUBARB PLANTING

Splitting an old crown of rhubarb for replanting.

Replanting a section of the old crown with the bud just above the surface.

A crown dug up for exposure to frost before forcing.

Forced rhubarb with traditional forcing pot on the left.

down in the autumn, cover the plants with a layer several inches thick of well-rotted manure or compost. Application of a nitrogen fertilizer in spring (see p. 11) will help to produce vigorous stems.

Provided the ground was relatively weed-free initially, little weeding is required as the large leaves tend to blanket the ground. The plants should remain productive for at least five seasons. When they are showing signs of decline, i.e. producing many thin stems, lift and divide the old crowns, replanting a few to maintain the crop. Replanting a few crowns each year is a sound policy.

The flowering heads which appear should be cut as they develop. Flowering is partly a varietal character, but it is also associated with wet summers, and with too high applications of nitrogen.

Harvesting/forcing

The first stems are normally ready in March or April, the season extending into May or June, depending on the variety.

For earlier production a few plants can be lifted in early winter. Unless there has been cold weather, roots should be dug up and left on the ground, exposed to low temperatures (to break their dormancy) before planting up under the greenhouse staging, or in pots or large boxes brought indoors. Light can be excluded to blanch the stems. Growth starts at temperatures of between 45° and 60 °F (7° and 16 °C). Forcing can also be done in black plastic sacks.

Alternatively, dormant crowns can be covered with rhubarb pots, etc. in December or January, tucking straw or dead leaves around the crowns. Or a thick layer of straw several inches thick can be put over the crowns to encourage earlier tender growth.

Diseases

Rhubarb may be attacked by honey fungus or crown rot, both of which kill the plants. Diseased plants should be dug up and burnt, and new stocks planted on a fresh site.

Some recommended cultivars

Early: Timperley Early, Hawkes Champagne.
Mid-season: Prince Albert.
Late: The Sutton, Victoria.

Salsify/Scorzonera

Salsify is a hardy biennial grown for its roots, which are creamy white and are used in winter. The young shoots (chards) of overwintered plants, and the mauve flower buds and flowering shoots are also edible.

Soil/situation

Salsify needs a relatively open situation. The roots develop best on deep, light, stone-free soil. The soil should have been manured for the previous crop.

Cultivation

Sow from March to May, ½ to ¾ inch deep (2 cm), in rows 6 inches apart (15 cm), aiming to get plants at 4 inches apart (10 cm). Use fresh seed as the viability of the seeds falls off rapidly. Keep the plants weeded and watered during the summer. The roots are ready for use from October onwards. For convenience or in very cold areas they can be lifted and stored in boxes (see p. 40), otherwise they can be left in the soil during the winter.

If chards are required, cut off the old leaves at about an inch above ground level (2.5 cm) in autumn, and earth up the roots with 5 to 6 inches of soil (15 cm). Well-blanched chards will be ready in spring. Alternatively cover the tops of the plants with at least 4 to 5 inches of straw, bracken or dry leaves (10–12 cm) when growth starts in spring.

If flower buds and flowering shoots are required leave a few plants in the soil to flower the following spring. Pick the buds with a few inches of stem just before they open.

SCORZONERA

Scorzonera is very similar to salsify, although it is a hardy perennial. The leaves are broader than salsify, the roots black skinned, and the flowers yellow.

Soil/situation/cultivation (See salsify)

Scorzonera is generally grown and used like salsify. However, being a perennial it can be left in the ground for a second season. Lift a few roots in the autumn, and if they are only pencil thick, leave the remainder in the ground until the following autumn. They will thicken up without toughening. Scorzonera can also be sown in August for use the following autumn.

SALSIFY

The spring-sown crop in July. Roots can be left in the ground in winter and lifted as required.

Roots lifted for cooking.

SCORZONERA

Plants growing in their first season (July). They can be left in the soil for a second season to grow larger.

Roots lifted for cooking.

Spinach and Leaf Beets

Several different vegetables are known or used as spinach. The true spinaches are annuals, which will seed in their first season. They are relatively small leaved. Round seeded spinach is used for a summer crop, and the hardier prickly seeded spinach for an overwintered crop.

The leaf beets belong to the beetroot family, but leaves, rather than the roots, are developed. They are hardy biennials, so do not normally run to seed in their first season. They are less susceptible to drought than true spinach, larger leaved, more prolific and robust, though perhaps less delicately flavoured. The group includes spinach beet or perpetual spinach, which looks like a dark, large-leaved spinach, and the Swiss chards, also known as seakale beet or silver chard. In the chards the leaf midrib and the leaf stalks are very swollen, and can be cut and used as a separate vegetable from the green parts of the leaf. The chards are robust, prolific and very handsome. Many forms have beautiful rose, red and silver coloured tints to the leaves, veins and stems. The best known of these is the red-stemmed Ruby Chard.

The third type of spinach is the half-hardy perennial, New Zealand spinach, a somewhat spiky leaved, succulent plant, which spreads over the ground. It grows well in dry soils and in hot conditions which are unsuitable for the other spinaches and leaf beets.

Site/soil

True spinach and leaf beets tolerate light shade. To grow well they need very fertile soil, rich in organic matter, well drained but moisture retentive. Poor soils which dry out should be avoided as they encourage premature bolting. The pH should be neutral to slightly alkaline: acid soils should be limed. They have high nitrogen requirements and respond to top-dressings of general fertilizer or sulphate of ammonia during growth (see p. 11).

They are best suited to the cool, moist conditions of spring and autumn, when they grow rapidly. They can be used for catch cropping and inter-cropping.

New Zealand spinach requires an open position. Although it grows well in moist, fertile soils, it is also very drought resistant and can grow in poorer dry soils without bolting.

SPINACH AND LEAF BEETS

Picking leaves of summer spinach.

Picking shoots of New Zealand spinach.

Cultivation

Summer spinach can be sown from late February (when soil conditions are suitable) until May. Small sowings can be made at 3-week intervals, sowing $\frac{1}{2}$ to $\frac{3}{4}$ inch deep (2 cm) in rows about a foot apart (30 cm); aim to have plants at 6 inches apart in the rows (15 cm). Such sowings can be picked from May until November, provided that they do not bolt prematurely due to hot or dry conditions.

Winter spinach is sown in August and September, in rows a foot apart (30 cm), spaced at 9 inches apart (22 cm). This will crop from November until the following spring. The quality of crop will be improved if it is cloched during the winter.

Leaf beet. The main sowings are made in March and April for crops during summer and winter; these plants frequently continue cropping until the following May or June. Sow in rows 15 to 18 inches apart (40–45 cm), with plants in the row 12 inches apart (30 cm).

A second sowing can be made in July or August. This will give lower yields, but will crop throughout the winter until the following summer.

Swiss chard: both the leaves and stalks are cooked.

Again, the overwintered crop will be of better quality if cloched during the winter.

The spinaches and leaf beets should always be sown as thinly as possible, and if necessary thinned to prevent overcrowding, which encourages mildew.

They can also be cultivated as cut-and-come-again crops, either by broadcasting or sowing very thinly at about 2 inches apart (5 cm), in rows 4 inches apart (10 cm). Cut off the young leaves just above ground level when 2 to 4 inches high (5–10 cm). Provided the soil is moist and fertile, several cuttings can be made.

New Zealand spinach. Seed can be sown indoors in April, hardened off, and planted out after risk of frost at the end of May, or sown directly outdoors in mid-May. Sow or transplant to about 18 inches apart (45 cm); the plants can easily cover a square yard of ground when mature. Seed is sometimes slow to germinate, and can be soaked in water overnight before sowing to hasten germination.

Harvesting

Spinach may be ready for use 10 to 12 weeks after sowing. With true spinach and leaf beets either individual leaves can be cut, or the whole plant can be cut about an inch above ground level (2.5 cm), leaving it to re-sprout. With New Zealand spinach a few young shoots should be taken from the base of the plant at each picking. The stem is discarded. Pick regularly or the leaves become tough.

Pests and diseases

The most common diseases of true spinach and leaf beet are downy mildew and leaf spots, usually due to poor drainage and lack of thinning (see p. viii). Birds are also a serious problem, sparrows in particular attacking all spinach and leaf beet, both at the young seedling stage and when plants are mature. Preventive measures should be taken when the seed is sown (see p. 46).

Some recommended cultivars

Summer spinach: Bloomsdale, Long Standing.
Winter spinach: Broad-leaved Prickly, Greenmarket.
Swiss chard: Lucullus.
Leaf beets such as perpetual spinach, and New Zealand spinach are rarely listed as named varieties.

Swedes and Turnips

Swedes are one of the hardiest of the root crops, and are grown mainly for winter use. They are milder and sweeter than turnips, and often succeed where turnips fail. The flesh is normally yellow, but in some cases white. The 'purple top' cultivars are considered best for home use.

Site/soil

Swedes need an open site, and do best on light, fertile soils, which suffer neither from waterlogging nor drought. The soil should be manured for the previous crop and limed if acid. Swedes belong to the brassica family, and must be rotated accordingly (see p. 44).

Cultivation

Swedes require a longer growing season than turnips, taking 20 to 26 weeks to mature. They are generally sown in late April or early May in the north, and late May and early June in the south. Sow in rows 15 to 18 inches apart (38–46 cm) and $\frac{1}{2}$ to $\frac{3}{4}$ inch deep (2 cm). Aim to get plants at 9 to 12 inches apart (23–30 cm), by sowing thinly and thinning later if necessary.

Apart from keeping the crop weed-free little attention is required (for fertilizer needs see p. 11). Growth will be checked if the soil is allowed to dry out, so watering will be needed in rainless periods, watering at the rate of 2 gal./sq. yd (22 litres/m^2) when necessary. This will improve the size and quality of the roots, but may reduce their flavour.

Harvesting

Roots are generally ready for use by September or October in the south and October or November in the north. They can be left in the ground until Christmas, but it is advisable to lift and store them then, or they become coarse and woody. They can be stored in clamps outdoors or in boxes under cover (see pp. 40–1).

Pests and diseases

The most frequent pest is flea beetle (see p. v). Other likely pests include mealy cabbage aphid (p. iv), cabbage root fly (p. v) and turnip gall weevil. The diseases clubroot and mildew are sometimes encountered (see p. vii). The new cultivar Marian has considerable resistance to both. Swedes are sometimes affected by various root rots, especially where grown for more than a year in one site. Burn diseased roots and practise rotation.

TURNIPS

Patch of turnip tops.

Some recommended cultivars

Best of All, Marian, Acme.

TURNIPS

Turnips are grown chiefly for their roots, which, by selecting appropriate cultivars, can be available for use all year round. Their 'tops' can also be used and make excellent spring greens. Turnips are flat, round or long in shape, with white or yellow flesh. Turnips are also brassicas, so need to be rotated accordingly (p. 44).

Site/soil

Turnips like cool moist conditions, and summer sowings can be made in light shade, provided there is plenty of moisture in the soil. Turnips have higher nitrogen requirements than swedes, particularly the early crops, so the soil should have plenty of organic matter worked in for the previous crop, or a top-dressing of general fertilizer applied before sowing (see p. 11).

Cultivation
Well-grown early turnips are a fast maturing crop, ready 10 to 12 weeks after sowing. They are useful for intercropping and catch cropping. Early maturing cultivars deteriorate rapidly once mature, and are best used when small. It is advisable to make successional sowings at 3-week intervals from early spring onwards. The hardy cultivars, grown for autumn use and storage, will stand longer without deteriorating.

The earliest sowings of summer turnips, using early cultivars, can be made under frames or cloches in February, followed by outdoor sowings in March and April; these will be ready in May and June. Turnips run to seed rapidly in dry weather, so sowings in May and June may not succeed if conditions are dry.

The main sowings of hardy cultivars for autumn and winter use and storage are made in July and August.

Sow turnips very thinly on a well-prepared seedbed, sowing seed at $\frac{3}{4}$ to 1 inch deep (2.5 cm). Sow early cultivars in rows 9 inches apart (22 cm), aiming to get plants at 4 inches apart (10 cm) in the rows, and winter cultivars in rows 12 inches apart (30 cm), with 6 inches between the plants (15 cm). Turnips grow very fast, so any necessary thinning must be done early, when the seedlings are no more than about an inch high (2.5 cm).

Turnips grown for tops are sown in August and September, or as early in spring as soil conditions allow, either under cover or in the open. Sow thinly in rows 6 inches apart (15 cm), or broadcast in a small patch. Use hardy cultivars for autumn sowings and early ones for spring sowings. Even if the seedlings are small at the start of winter, they will make rapid growth in spring. The first cutting can be made when the seedlings are between 5 and 6 inches high (15 cm), about an inch above ground level. If left longer they become tough. Provided the ground is not allowed to dry out, several further cuttings can be made before the plants run to seed. This crop is particularly useful in early spring after a hard winter.

Watering, pests and diseases See Swedes.

Harvesting
Early cultivars of turnips will be ready when about $1\frac{1}{2}$ to 2 inches (5 cm) in diameter. Hardy turnips can be left in the soil until Christmas, then stored as for swedes (see p. 40). Being less hardy than swedes, they need a soil covering if clamped.

Some recommended cultivars
Early: Snowball, Tokyo Cross F_1.
Hardy: Golden Ball, Golden Perfection (both yellow fleshed), Manchester Market (Green Top Stone).

SWEDE AND TURNIP TYPES

Left to right, swede, white-fleshed Snowball turnip, yellow-fleshed Golden Ball turnip.

THINNING TURNIPS

Thinning turnips when growing for roots.

Sweet Corn

This is a tender crop which needs a long growing season. It is unlikely to do well in the north of the British Isles, although plant breeders are continually producing cultivars more tolerant of low temperatures.

Site/soil

Avoid an exposed position, choosing a warm sheltered site. Sweet corn grows best on deep, well-drained, reasonably fertile and slightly acid soils. Avoid very dry soils and heavy clays. The soil is best manured for the previous crop; otherwise apply a base dressing before sowing or planting (see p. 11).

Sweet corn can be undercropped with crops such as marrows, courgettes, french beans or salad plants.

Cultivation

Sweet corn will not germinate at soil temperatures below 50 °F (10 °C), which are not normally reached until about the end of May in the south, and two weeks later in the north. Plants are checked by transplanting and cannot be planted out until risk of frost is past. Therefore the most satisfactory way of raising plants is to sow seed in gentle heat indoors, in soil blocks or small pots, during April. Sow 2 to 3 seeds per block or pot, 1 to 1½ inches deep (3 to 4 cm), thinning to one seedling after germination. Harden off well before planting out in late May or early June. Plant out under cloches if possible.

Sweet corn can also be sown directly outdoors during May but will not crop as early as the transplanted crops. Sow under cloches or individual jam jars (removing them when they are outgrown), or cover the seedbed with clear plastic film to raise the soil temperature. Slits can be cut in the film to pull the young seedlings through when germinated. Sow 2 to 3 seeds per site, thinning to one after germination. It is advisable to use dressed seed for outdoor sowings to protect seedlings from frit fly. Sweet corn is also a good subject for fluid sowing (see pp. 24–5).

Sweet corn is wind pollinated. Each of the 'silks' on the female flower has to be pollinated to get a well-filled cob. To help pollination sweet corn should be planted in a block formation, spacing the plants either at 14 inches apart (35 cm) each way, or at 10 to 12 inches apart (25–30 cm) in rows about 2 feet apart (60 cm).

When plants are between 12 and 18 inches high (30–45 cm) the stems can be earthed up to make them more stable. Alternatively they can be tied to

PLANTING SWEET CORN

Planting out pot-raised sweet corn at the end of May (in the south).

Earthing up the plants in mid-June.

Young plants grown in block formation to help cross-pollination.

canes. They should be hoed very shallowly in the early stages, or the root system will be damaged. Mulching will help to control weeds and conserve moisture in the soil.

Little watering is necessary until flowering begins and later when the grains are swelling. At these stages regular watering every few days at the rate of 4 gal./sq. yd (22 litres/m^2) increases both yield quality and quantity.

Harvesting

Each plant normally produces only one or two cobs and these are ready from July to October, depending on cultivar. There is a tendency in this country to harvest cobs when they are over-mature. They are more tender and digestible when picked rather earlier. An indication of ripeness is the cob tassel turning brown. If a finger-nail is pressed into a kernel, the juice inside is milky when mature, watery when under-ripe, and doughy when over-mature. Cobs should be snapped off just before required, as sweetness in older cultivars is rapidly lost after picking.

The extra-sweet modern cultivars, such as Extra Early Sweet, retain their sweetness for up to a week after picking. They should be planted away from older cultivars, or this characteristic will be lost by cross-pollination.

Pests

Frit fly is the most likely pest (see p. vi). Slugs can be damaging in the early stages (see p. iv). Birds sometimes uproot seedlings; in this case put strong black cotton over the rows (see p. 46).

Some recommended cultivars

Sweet corn cultivars are grouped as early, mid or late season. The earlier the cultivar the shorter the growing season. Only the early types are likely to succeed further north.

Early: Earliking F_1, Extra Early Sweet F_1, John Innes Hybrid, Kelvedon Sweetheart F_1, Seneca Pathfinder.

Mid: Aztec F_1, Kelvedon Glory F_1, Northern Belle F_1, Seneca Beauty.

Late: Jubilee, October Gold.

HARVESTING SWEET CORN

The cob at the brown tassel stage: ready to pick.

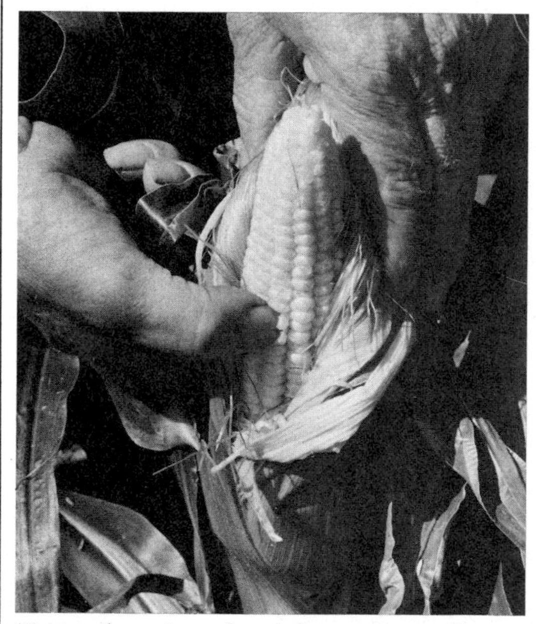

Testing the grain on the cob for maturity: milky juice exuding from the grain indicates ripeness.

Sweet Peppers

The sweet or green pepper, which has become increasingly popular in this country, is the immature fruit of the annual capsicum. Depending on variety, it turns red, yellow, or even purple black when fully mature. The commonest shape is a somewhat rectangular bell, but there are long forms, either narrow or broad, and squat, tomato-shaped forms. The hot chili types are very variable.

Site/soil

Sweet peppers need high light intensity and warmth. Only in milder parts of the country can they be grown outdoors unprotected. In most areas they crop far more reliably if grown in frames, or, for the early stages at least, under cloches. They can also be grown in large pots of at least 8 inches diameter (20 cm) or in growing bags.

The outdoor crop should be in a warm sheltered position. The soil needs to be fertile and moisture retentive, but not freshly manured.

Cultivation

The early fruiting F_1 hybrid cultivars are the most reliable for indoor and outdoor cropping in this country.

Sow indoors in March or early April for the outdoor crop. Sow the seed ½ to ¾ inch deep (2 cm) in gentle heat if possible, in soil blocks or seed trays. Alternatively sow two to three seeds in a small pot, thinning to one seedling. Pricking out is done at the three-leaf stage into 2- or 3-inch pots (5–8 cm).

They are ready for planting into large pots, or into their permanent positions outdoors, when the first flowers are showing or when they are about 4 to 5 inches high (10–12 cm). Before planting outside towards the end of May or early June harden off well. Delay planting if there is any risk of frost or if the soil is cold. Wherever possible plant out under cloches.

The aim with peppers should be to produce sturdy, bushy plants. If growth is spindly and weak, nip out the growing point when the plants are about 18 inches high (45 cm). If growth is vigorous the plants will need to be staked like outdoor tomatoes (see p. 135). It is important not to let the soil dry out during growth, and regular watering will be needed in dry spells; plants in the open ground benefit from being mulched.

When the first terminal flower appears, it may be left to develop a fruit or removed. A decision depends on the plant's growth state: if it is growing

SWEET PEPPERS

Planting out a sweet pepper, with the flowers just showing.

With the removal of the first central fruit the side ones will develop.

vigorously leave the "king" flower to develop, which will help to balance excess vegetative growth. But, if the plant is growing slowly, remove the king flower so that lateral shoots are encouraged to develop.

Once the fruits have started to swell regular liquid feeding with a tomato fertilizer every week or fortnight is beneficial.

Chili peppers are grown in the same way as sweet peppers.

Harvesting

Cropping normally starts in July indoors and August outdoors, and will continue until frost. Picking can start when the first fruits are the size of a tennis ball, and be continued regularly to encourage further cropping. Peppers will only turn red if left on the plant for a long period in a warm season. If frost seems likely towards the end of the season the whole plant can be uprooted and hung indoors in a frost-free place. Sweet peppers will keep in good condition on the plant for several months.

Pests and diseases

The outdoor crop is relatively trouble free.

Some recommended cultivars for outdoor use

Ace F_1, Canapé F_1, Early Prolific F_1.

TYPES OF PEPPERS

Top row, left to right, Early Prolific, bell and block types. Below, chili types.

Outdoor Tomatoes

Tomatoes, being half hardy, require long warm summers to fruit well. In most years a satisfactory crop can be grown outdoors, especially in the south of England; chances of success are greatly improved all over the country if the crop is protected with cloches or frames.

Tomato cultivars are either tall or bushy in form. Tall cultivars need staking or support, as well as removal of side branches (see below). Bush cultivars remain small compact plants, and require no staking or sideshooting. They tend to fruit earlier and to have a shorter productive season; they are useful for outdoor crops especially under cloches.

Site/soil

A sheltered site is essential for tomatoes, ideally backed by a south-facing wall, provided the soil is not allowed to dry out. Erect an artificial windbreak if the site is exposed. Soil should be fertile, well drained and moisture retentive. Fork in plenty of well-rotted manure or compost beforehand. A basic fertilizer can be applied before planting (see p. 11). Where tomatoes are grown in pots use John Innes No. 3 potting compost, or the equivalent. Growing bags are also useful for tomatoes. Tomatoes are subject to many of the same diseases as potatoes and if grown in the open garden should be rotated accordingly.

Cultivation

Sow in gentle heat indoors from mid-March to early April. Tomatoes require a minimum soil temperature of 50 °F (10 °C) to germinate, but the seedlings can afterwards withstand lower temperatures provided that day temperatures rise above 61 °F (16 °C) to 'repair' any damage. Either sow in seed trays and prick out into 2- or 3-inch pots, or sow 2 or 3 seeds directly into small pots, thinning to one per pot after germination. Plants will be ready for planting out 6 to 8 weeks after sowing, at the end of May or early June. Harden off thoroughly before planting. The first flowering truss should be visible at planting.

Plants for transplanting can be raised cheaply by fluid sowing in a frame in early April, in rows 4 inches apart (10 cm), aiming to space plants at 1½ inches apart (3.5 cm). These will be ready for planting out in mid- to late May when 6 to 8 inches high (15–20 cm). (See p. 134.)

Alternatively plants can be bought, though the choice of cultivar is usually limited. Select stocky

TOMATOES

Planting out the tomato; the first flowers are just open.

A tall type of tomato, needs to be staked.

Cutting out the terminal shoot above the fourth flower truss.

Plants are cut from their stakes and laid on straw at the end of summer for ripening the last fruits.

Side shoots are removed from a tall tomato variety.

Bush tomato plants, strawed down to keep the fruits clean.

plants, preferably in individual pots rather than in boxes, to minimize the transplanting setback.

Plant tall cultivars about 15 inches apart (37 cm), and bush cultivars 12 to 19 inches apart (30–45 cm). The closer spacing gives earlier yields; the wider spacing higher total yields in good summers. Plant under cloches or in frames if available, so that the plants have a more stable environment in which to become established.

Fluid sowing can be used for direct sowing of outdoor tomatoes, using certain bush cultivars such as Sleaford Abundance and Arla, which will give an early crop.

Pre-germinated seed is sown under cloches in mid-April (having left the cloches in position for several days beforehand to warm up the soil), or in the open at the end of April. Aim to space the seeds at 2 to 3 per foot of row. These plants should start cropping in August.

Tall cultivars of tomatoes need to be supported with a 4 foot (1.2 m) cane or stake put in at the time of planting. Bush cultivars need to be mulched with plastic to keep the fruit clean. Plants may be grown under cloches after transplanting but these need to be removed at flowering time to allow for pollination.

With tall cultivars the side shoots must be removed as they appear in the axils of the leaves. To ensure that most of the crop matures and ripens before the end of the growing season, plants also have to be 'stopped', i.e. the growing point removed, after 3 trusses have set in the north of England and after 4 or 5 in the south. This is generally done in late July or early August, at one or two leaves above the top truss of flowers.

Once outdoor tomatoes are established watering is not usually required until flowering starts. From this stage onwards and in dry weather, plants benefit from fairly heavy watering, at the rate of at least 2 gal./sq. yd (11 litres/m^2) per week. This gives higher yields of larger fruits but may dilute their flavour.

Tomatoes grown in pots or growing bags need regular watering throughout their growth. Irregular watering often results in 'blossom end rot', a disorder in which sunken rotten patches appear at the end of the fruit (see p. iii).

The outdoor crop normally requires no supplementary feeding unless grown in pots or growing bags, when liquid feeding with a tomato fertilizer is recommended (follow the manufacturer's recommendations). Bush tomatoes should not have too much nitrogen or they will make leaf growth at the expense of fruit production.

Remove withered and diseased leaves from the plants during the growing season and burn them.

Harvesting

The outdoor crop is normally ready about the second half of August. Pick fruit as ripe as possible to get the best flavour. In late September plants can be cut down from the stakes where they stand, and covered with cloches to ripen off the remaining fruit. Otherwise uproot the plants and hang them by their roots in a greenhouse or indoors for the fruit to ripen slowly. Fruits can also be picked off the plants, wrapped in soft paper, and put in a drawer or warm cupboard to ripen: they can also be cut with 3 or 4 inches of stem (10 cm), like grapes, so they can be hung between two horizontal canes to ripen.

Pests, diseases and disorders

Damping off in the seedling stage (p. vi), botrytis, stemrot (p. viii), potato blight (pp. iii, viii) and potato mosaic virus (p. viii) are the most serious diseases outdoors. There are few pests outdoors, other than potato cyst eelworm (see p. vi) and occasionally whitefly.

Tomatoes are very easily affected by hormone weedkillers (such as 2,4-D), so make it a rule that the plants are not watered using a container earlier used for applying weedkiller. Affected plants show spirally twisted stems and leaves. They may recover, but the fruits produced are usually of poor quality.

Plants fed with a fertilizer containing a high potash level, frequently show symptoms of magnesium deficiency (see p. iii). The signs start with the lower leaves becoming orange-yellow between the veins and this spreads up to the upper leaves. Affected plants are treated with foliar sprays of magnesium sulphate at 7- to 10-day intervals, at a rate of 8 oz. in 2½ gal. of water (225 g in 11 litres) plus a spreader such as soft soap, which will help the spray to stick to the foliage.

Some recommended cultivars

Bush varieties: Sleaford Abundance F_1, Alfresco F_1, Amateur, Arla, Pixie, Sigmabush, French Cross F_1. *Tall varieties for outdoor or indoor use:* Ailsa Craig, Alicante, Gardeners' Delight (Sugar Plum), Golden Sunrise (yellow), Harbinger, Marmande, Moneycross, Ronoclave, Sweet 100.

Salad Plants

The following are brief notes on the cultivation of some of the traditional, low-growing plants often known as 'salad herbs', as they were used mainly in salads. Most are winter hardy, and particularly useful in autumn, winter and early spring.

Those marked ** can be left in the open in winter, but if protected with cloches the quality of the crop is improved greatly and they will start into growth again much earlier in spring.

Claytonia (winter purslane).** This is a hardy annual with very pretty succulent, heart-shaped leaves. It will grow on poor soils and in shaded positions, and is most useful in spring when it grows very rapidly. Sow in July and August for winter use, and in April and May for summer. Sow very thinly in rows about 12 inches apart (30 cm), the plants 6 inches apart (15 cm). The leaves, flowering stalks and flowers are all edible. The plant re-sprouts several times after cutting.

Corn salad (lamb's lettuce).** A hardy annual with small, mild-flavoured leaves, corn salad withstands very low temperatures and is a useful lettuce substitute in winter and early spring. It will grow in most soils and situations. Main sowings for winter use are made in July and August, sowing on a firm seedbed either broadcast, or in rows about 6 inches apart (15 cm), the plants about 4 inches apart (10 cm). A second sowing can be made in March and April for summer use. Pick off a few leaves at a time from each plant.

American or land cress.** This is a hardy biennial with shiny green, deeply indented leaves, with a very strong watercress flavour. It does best in fairly rich soils, and tolerates moist soil and shady positions. The summer crop is best grown in light shade. Sow in July and August for supplies from autumn to spring; and in March to June for a summer crop. Space the rows about 8 inches apart (20 cm) and plants about 6 inches apart (15 cm). Pick individual leaves as required.

Mediterranean rocket (Italian cress).** This fairly hardy, sharply flavoured annual survives most English winters in the open. It can be grown all year round, but tends to run to seed rapidly and become very strongly flavoured in hot dry conditions. It can be used either in the seedling stage as a broadcast crop (see p. 138), cutting when about 2 inches high

SALAD PLANTS

Mustard and cress

Winter purslane (Claytonia)

Summer purslane

Corn salad

(5 cm), or sown in rows 8 inches apart (20 cm), the plants spaced up to 6 inches apart for larger plants (15 cm). Main sowings are made from August to October for the autumn to early spring crop. It can also be sown from March to June for the summer crop.

Summer purslane. This is a half-hardy succulent, mild-flavoured plant with green or golden fleshy leaves. It needs a warm sheltered position to grow well, and does best on light, well-drained soils. Sow indoors in April, or direct outdoors in May and June, at about 6 inches apart (15 cm). Keep picking the young shoots, always leaving two leaves at the base of the stem to encourage further growth. Do not allow the plants to flower, or the foliage will become tough. The leaves and stems are edible.

Mustard and cress. This can either be grown in dishes indoors or in soil outdoors. When grown indoors line a dish with blotting paper or flannel to retain moisture, and sow the seed evenly on this base. To encourage growth it can be started in the dark and moved into the light when seedlings are about an inch high (2.5 cm). Seedlings must be kept moist throughout growth. Mustard normally germinates faster than cress so if both are required it should be sown 3 days earlier, either in the same or a separate dish. Milder flavoured rape is sometimes substituted for mustard.

Mustard and cress can be sown broadcast outdoors, and treated as a seedling crop (see p. 137). Cress is less coarse growing than mustard or rape, and more suitable for growing outdoors. Sowings should only be made in spring and late summer or autumn, as they tend to run to seed in hot weather. Spring and autumn sowings can be cut up to 5 times if the soil remains moist. An extremely useful sowing can be made under cloches or in frames, in February or early March.

SALAD PLANTS

American or land cress

Mediterranean rocket

Culinary Herbs

As there are many specialist books on herbs, only brief notes on some of the most useful culinary herbs are included here (for chives and parsley see pp. 108 and 111). Most herbs can be easily bought as young plants.

Basil (*Ocimum basilicum*) is a tender Mediterranean herb with a clove-like flavour. It grows best under cloches, in a frame or greenhouse. Sow in March or April, planting out under cover in May or outside after risk of frost, about 5 inches apart (15 cm). A second sowing can be made in June and July and the plants potted up to bring indoors for use during the winter.

Chervil (*Anthriscus cerefolium*) is a rapidly growing hardy annual, rather like parsley in appearance, with an aniseed flavour. It can be available all year round, remaining green in winter. The summer crop should be grown in a shady position in fertile moisture-retentive soil. The winter crop is best in a sunny position or under cover. Sow February to April for summer use and in August for the autumn to spring crop. Thin or plant to about 4 inches apart (10 cm). Seedlings can be transplanted into a cold greenhouse or frame in September or October to give fresh supplies during the winter.

Marjoram (*Origanum* spp.). The marjorams have a very pleasant characteristic flavour. They grow best in good soil in a sunny position. Sweet or knotted marjoram is treated as an annual, and is sown indoors in March or outdoors in April or May, eventually thinning or planting about 7 inches apart (15 cm). Pot marjoram is hardier and perennial; it can be raised from seed or softwood cuttings taken in early summer or by dividing plants in autumn. Trim foliage back in autumn.

Mint. Very many types of mint are cultivated, the commonest culinary mints being ordinary spearmint (*Mentha* × *spicata*), and two soft, round-leaved mints, apple (*M. suaveolens*) and Bowles' (*M.* × *villosa alopecuroides*). They require rich, moist, weed-free soil, and should be moved every 3 or 4 years as they exhaust the soil. The site needs to be well prepared beforehand, working in well-rotted manure or compost. Plant either young shoots with

CULINARY HERBS

Sage

Basil, sweet

roots, or pieces of root, preferably in March or early April. Plant about 9 inches apart (22 cm), laying the pieces of root horizontally about 2 inches deep (5 cm). All types of mint normally die back in winter. After 3 or 4 years lift the plants in autumn, divide them and replant in a fresh site.

Sage (*Salvia officinalis*) is a perennial bushy plant which does best on light well-drained soil. It can be raised from seed sown in spring, or by taking heel or tip cuttings in May. Plant young plants or rooted cuttings in spring about 2 inches apart (5 cm). If the lower parts of the bush are earthed up in spring, the covered shoots will produce roots which can be separated off and planted out. Cut the young growths back lightly in July after flowering to keep the bushes compact.

Savory (*Satureja* spp.). The savories are strongly flavoured herbs. Summer savory is a tender annual, and likes rich soil and a sunny position. It is sown outdoors in April, thinning to about 6 inches apart (15 cm). Winter savory is perennial, and can be grown on poor soil, provided it is well drained. Seed can be also sown in spring, or in a frame in August or September, planting out the following spring. It can be raised more quickly from heel cuttings taken in spring, or by the division of old plants in March. Winter savory can be potted up in late summer for use indoors in winter.

Thyme (*Thymus* spp.). There are many varieties of thyme, common, lemon scented and caraway being the most used for culinary purposes. They are low-growing bushy perennials and like dry, well-drained, sunny positions. They can be propagated either by sowing seed in spring, planting out the seedlings about a foot apart (30 cm), by taking cuttings in April or May, or by dividing old plants, the last 2 methods giving usable plants sooner. Thyme tends to become straggly and woody after 3 or 4 years, and should then be replaced.

CULINARY HERBS

Basil, bush

Chervil

Month-by-month in the vegetable garden

The following list is intended as a reminder of the principal jobs in season. It is based on average conditions, in the southern half of England: allowance must always be made for weather and locality. In mild districts spring sowings and plantings can often be done earlier, and autumn sowings and planting later than those given. In the north and in colder areas the reverse is the case.

Sow under cover means sowing in frames, cloches or tunnels, or in a frost-free greenhouse.

JANUARY

Clear, dig and manure land, if not too wet.

Order the year's seeds and seed potatoes.

Sort through stored vegetables, and remove those rotting.

Cover rhubarb for forcing.

Force witloof chicory and **blanch** endives.

Lift for use: jerusalem artichokes, celeriac, parsnips, winter radishes.

Harvest: brussels sprouts, leaf beets, winter cabbage (including savoys), celery, leeks, kales, winter salads.

Use from store: beetroots, white cabbages, carrots, marrows, onions and shallots, potatoes, swedes and turnips.

FEBRUARY

Sow (with heat): summer cabbages and cauliflowers, celeriac, celery, leeks and onions.

Sow under cover: beetroots, broad beans, brussels sprouts, abyssinian cabbages, carrots, cauliflowers, lettuces, bulb and spring onions, radishes, peas (south only), spinach and turnips.

Force witloof chicory and **blanch** endives.

Start setting out seed potatoes for chitting.

Top dress overwintered Japanese onions.

Dig and manure light ground, unless wet or frozen: start preparing seedbeds for early sowing and plantings.

Lift or use from store: jerusalem artichokes, carrots, celeriac, parsnips, winter radishes.

Harvest: brussels sprouts, savoy cabbages, leaf beets, kales, purple sprouting broccoli, winter salads.

MARCH

Sow (with heat): aubergines, celery, celeriac, sweet peppers, tomatoes.

Sow under cover: cauliflower, carrots, celery, celeriac, leeks, lettuces.

Sow in the open: beetroot and leaf beets, broad beans, brussels sprouts, summer cabbages, carrots, calabrese, celery, corn salad, kales, lettuces, leeks, onions, parsley, parsnips, peas, radishes, salsify, scorzonera, summer spinach and turnips.

Plant out: globe and jerusalem artichokes, asparagus, early summer cabbages and cauliflowers, lettuces, onion sets, shallots, early potatoes.

Lift or use from store: jerusalem artichokes, carrots, celeriac, parnsips, winter radishes.

Harvest: brussels sprouts, spring and savoy cabbages, kales, sprouting broccoli, rhubarb, winter salads.

APRIL

Sow under cover: aubergines, french and runner beans, celery, celeriac, cucumbers, marrows, New Zealand spinach, sweet corn, sweet peppers, tomatoes.

Sow in the open: beetroots, leaf beets, brussels sprouts, sprouting broccoli, summer and winter cabbages, calabrese, carrots, cauliflowers, kales, kohl rabi, leeks, lettuces, onions (all types), parsley, parsnips, peas, radishes, salsify, scorzonera, summer spinach, turnips.

Plant out: globe and jerusalem artichokes, asparagus, brussels sprouts, spring cabbages, cauliflowers, lettuces, onion sets, early and maincrop potatoes.

Hoe and weed all crops.

Uproot and burn old stumps of brassicas.

Earth up early potatoes.

Prepare celery trench.

Harvest: asparagus, leaf beets, sprouting broccoli, spring cabbages, kales, rhubarb, spring greens, turnips, winter cauliflowers: and lettuces and radishes from frames.

MAY

Sow under cover (early May): cucumbers, marrows, sweet corn.

Sow in the open: french and runner beans, beetroots, sprouting broccoli, brussels sprouts, summer and winter cabbages, calabrese, carrots, cauliflowers, kales, kohl rabi, land cress, lettuces, spring and pickling onions, parsley, maincrop peas, radishes, salsify, scorzonera, summer and New Zealand spinaches, swedes: and (end May) cucumbers, marrows, sweet corn.

Plant under protection (later removed): cucumbers, marrows, sweet corn, tomatoes.

MAY

Plant in open: brussels sprouts, french and runner beans, summer and winter cabbage, celery, celeriac, leeks.

Keep hoeing and weeding.

Earth up potatoes.

Stake peas.

Watch out for signs of attacks by blackfly on broad beans, of carrot fly, of cabbage root fly, of flea beetle, of onion fly, taking preventive measures as necessary.

Harvest: asparagus, leaf beets, sprouting broccoli, spring cabbages, lettuces, radishes, spring onions, winter cauliflowers.

JUNE

Sow in open: french and runner beans, beetroots, leaf beets, calabrese, carrots, chicories (all types), Chinese cabbages, cucumbers, endives, kohl rabi, lettuces, marrows, peas, radishes, summer and New Zealand spinach, swedes, sweet corn, turnips.

Plant out: aubergines, brussels sprouts, sprouting broccoli, summer and winter cabbages, cauliflowers, celery, celeriac, kales, leeks, marrows, peppers, tomatoes, sweet corn.

Keep hoeing, weeding and mulching.

Watch out for pests (as in May) and take necessary action.

Harvest: asparagus, broad and french beans, beetroot, leaf beet, cabbage, calabrese, carrots, cauliflower, kohl rabi, lettuce, salad onions, overwintered Japanese onions, peas, early potatoes, radish, rhubarb, summer spinach, turnips.

JULY

Sow in open: dwarf french beans, beetroots, leaf beets, spring cabbages (end July in north only), carrots, red and sugar loaf chicories, chinese cabbages, endives, kohl rabi, autumn lettuces, spring onions, parsley, peas (early dwarf cvs only), summer and winter radishes, winter spinach, winter salads, turnips (for storage).

Plant out: sprouting broccoli, brussels sprouts, autumn and winter cabbages, calabrese, late cauliflowers, kales, leeks.

Keep weeding, hoeing and mulching.

Tie, remove side-shoots and take out the top of staked tomatoes (after 4 to 5 trusses have formed).

Earth up brassicas and stake in exposed sites.

Water, when necessary, globe artichokes, celeriac, celery, cucumbers, leeks, marrows, beans.

JULY

Spray maincrop potatoes against blight in warm humid weather.

Watch out for pests and take necessary action.

Harvest: globe artichokes, broad, french and runner beans, beetroots, leaf beets, cabbages, calabrese, carrots, self-blanching celery, courgettes, cucumbers, endives, kohl rabi, lettuces, leeks, marrows, spring and maincrop onions, peas, early potatoes, radishes, shallots, summer spinach, sweet corn, turnips.

AUGUST

Sow in open: leaf beets, spring cabbages (first two weeks in August in south), chinese cabbages, endive, fennel (early iugust), winter lettuces, spring, Japanese and traditional overwintering onions, parsley, summer and winter radishes, winter spinach, turnips, winter salads.

Sow (for later cloching): beetroots, carrots, endives, winter lettuces.

Plant out: sprouting broccoli, winter cabbages, winter cauliflowers, kales (all early in August), leeks.

Hoe regularly between crops, and **water** when necessary.

Stop staked tomatoes when 4 or 5 flower trusses have been formed: spray against blight in warm, humid weather.

Earth up and stake brassicas.

Lift and dry off onions.

Harvest: globe artichokes, broad, french and runner beans, beetroots, leaf beets, cabbages, calabrese, carrots, self-blanching celery, courgettes, cucumbers, endives, kohl rabi, lettuces, leeks, marrows, spring and maincrop onions, peas, early potatoes, radishes, shallots, summer spinach, sweet corn, turnips, plus outdoor aubergines and peppers in favourable areas.

SEPTEMBER

Sow in open: spring and red cabbages, endives, lettuces (for overwintering as seedlings), radish, winter spinach, turnips (for tops).

Plant out: spring cabbages, winter lettuces.

Earth up winter brassicas.

Cut down outdoor tomatoes and finish ripening indoors or under cloches on straw.

Cut off and burn potato haulm if infected by blight.

Cut marrows and bring in to store before frost.

SEPTEMBER

Earth up trench celery.

Cover with cloches late sowings of dwarf beans, carrots, endives, lettuces and radishes in mid-September.

Harvest: globe artichokes, aubergines, broad, french and runner beans, beetroots, leaf beets, cabbages, calabrese, carrots, self-blanching celery, chicories, chinese cabbages, courgettes, cucumbers, endives, kohl rabi, lettuces, leeks, marrows, spring and maincrop onions, peas, maincrop potatoes, radishes, shallots, summer spinach, sweet corn, sweet peppers, swedes and turnips.

OCTOBER

Sow under cover: summer cauliflowers, winter lettuces.

Sow in the open: broad beans, peas (hardy cvs).

Plant out: leaf beets, spring cabbages, winter lettuces, onion sets (overwintering cvs), rhubarb.

Lift and store: beetroots, carrots, winter cabbages, potatoes and turnips.

Start blanching endives.

Lift, trim and store witloof chicory for forcing as required.

Earth up leeks and celery.

Cut down asparagus fern and jerusalem artichoke.

Protect late cauliflowers from frost by covering curd, and parsley, herbs and winter salads with cloches and low tunnels.

Clear away pea sticks, bean supports, general debris.

Start digging and manuring: apply lime where necessary.

Harvest: brussels sprouts, french and runner beans, leaf beets, cabbages, cauliflowers, carrots, celeriac, trench celery, chinese cabbages, lettuces, parsnips, peas, radishes, summer and winter spinach, winter salads, swedes, sweet corn.

NOVEMBER

Sow in open: broad beans, peas.

Plant out rhubarb.

Lift and store: late-sown beetroots, carrots, turnips, swedes.

Continue blanching endive and forcing witloof chicory.

Earth up celery.

Protect celeriac and globe artichokes from frost with bracken.

Cover with straw root crops to be wintered in the ground.

Continue to clear debris, and to dig and manure.

Check stored vegetables and remove any which have rotted.

Harvest: jerusalem artichokes, leaf beets, brussels sprouts, winter cabbages, cauliflowers, celeriac, celery, kales, leeks, protected lettuces, parsnips, winter radishes, salsify and scorzonera, swedes, winter salads.

DECEMBER

Lift and store late-sown carrots and swedes.

Continue blanching endive and forcing witloof chicory.

Continue to remove debris, and to dig, manure and lime vacant ground.

Cover rhubarb crowns for forcing; or lift for forcing indoors.

Gather and use from store: beetroots, carrots, witloof chicory, marrows, potatoes, shallots, and turnips.

Index